CREATING
SPACE

Bryan D. Sims & Craig W. Robertson

CREATING
SPACE

Cultivating Environments for
Disciples of Jesus to Thrive and Multiply

 invite
PRESS
Plano, Texas

CREATING SPACE:
Cultivating Environments for Disciples of Jesus to Thrive and Multiply

Copyright © 2024 by Bryan D. Sims and Craig W. Robertson

Spiritual Leadership, Inc. (SLI)

http://www.spiritual-leadership.org/

This book is printed on acid-free, elemental chlorine-free paper.

ISBN Paperback 978-1-963265-33-0; eBook 978-1-963265-28-6

All scripture quotations unless noted otherwise are taken from the New Revised Standard Version of the Bible, copyright 1989, Division of Christian Education of the National Council of the Churches of Christ in the United States of America. Used by permission. All rights reserved.

Scripture quotations marked NIV are taken from THE HOLY BIBLE, NEW INTERNATIONAL VERSION®, NIV® Copyright © 1973, 1978, 1984, 2011 by Biblica, Inc.™ Used by permission of Zondervan. All rights reserved worldwide.

24 25 26 27 28 29 30 31 32 33 —10 9 8 7 6 5 4 3 2 1

MANUFACTURED in the UNITED STATES of AMERICA

To the many leaders, teams, and churches whom we have had the privilege to walk alongside in the past couple of decades. May you see the generative fruitfulness of more than you can imagine in Christ as the Spirit works in and through you to the glory of God (Ephesians 3:20).

CONTENTS

Chapter 4

PROLOGUE

Over the last twenty-five years a shift in perceptions of the North American church has occurred. It has become evident that there has been a transition from perceiving it as essentially stable to acknowledging its decline in the face of a growing secular culture. This shift is significant because it renders general diagnostics ineffective in generating the necessary impetus for change. Both laity and clergy commonly express dissatisfaction with the state of the church, often ascribing to it a long list of issues needing attention. Engaging in general discussions allows individuals to avoid a sense of responsibility, fostering a mindset that nothing can be done and that it is not their responsibility.

The ability to shift conversations from generalities to specifics is crucial in identifying root causes and strategies that can ignite the passions of the gifted. Without this transition, the risk remains that individuals stay on the sidelines, contributing to a world marked by increasing pain and suffering. The observation that patterns of the world might lead to heightened desperation emphasizes the urgency of addressing issues at their core. The good news is that once people begin to see themselves as an essential part of God's plan and begin to find spaces where they can dream about their contribution with others, they find passion and energy to live out a deeper sense of purpose or calling.

During the Babylonian exile and again during the Roman era, drawing insights from other civilizations to avert potential uprisings that could undermine the government, laws were instituted to regulate public gatherings. The regulations permitted citizens to organize around any topic, provided they adhered to a set of rules. These guidelines mandated preplanned gatherings where an individual took the responsibility of addressing the public. The roots of our contemporary Sunday worship services can be traced back to these historical contexts. The underlying idea is that by designating a primary spokesperson, the authorities aimed to alleviate the burden of responsibility on individuals, preventing the grassroots empowerment that could fuel a movement.[1]

I (Craig) remember walking through the streets of Nuremburg, Germany, not that many years after the Allied forces had bombed most of the city into rubble. I thought it was strange to be an American walking those streets by myself without any hint that I was out of place. I was there to work with a church that was in the heart of the city, and we were on a break from the work of leadership. That morning the team of people were listing the context (specific realities) of their situation so they could build strategies that would connect with the people they were serving. As I walked along, ducking into little stores, I could see the same expressions that I would see in any city—laughter, anger, concern, wonder. It was so familiar. A question bubbled up that I took with me back to the meeting with the church. I shared with them an assumption that everyone could tell I was an American just by looking at me. They smiled with an affirmation. Then I asked them, "Why was it okay for me to walk around here after the ter-

---

1. Alan Kreider, *The Patient Ferment of the Early Church: The Improbable Rise of Christianity in the Roman Empire* (Grand Rapids, MI: Baker Academic, 2016).

rible things that have happened?" They explained that as a culture they had allowed the Nazi regime to gain power, that they had not been willing to step into the arena and risk specific strategies to prevent what they knew in their hearts to be wrong. In a word, the people of this city had been having general conversations and assumed that specific ideas of how to overcome the situation were not plausible. They had been inoculated from using their gifts and creativity in the world.

Our hope in these pages is to create spaces/environments where together, people can explore how God's unique design of their life intersects with the world in which they are participating. This environment we are aiming at is a safe place where people can talk about the specifics of their journey with others as it intersects the gospel and the timeless principles of abiding in Christ. We are witness to the loving, risk-taking, and transformational effects of a people who are truly Passionate Spiritual Disciples (PSDs).

Our journeys are both unique and normal. While we work together to help lead an organization devoted to creating transforming environments for Passionate Spiritual Disciples and Passionate Spiritual Leaders,[2] our backgrounds are quite diverse. Bryan grew up in church and has spent most of his adult life serving in ministry roles of one sort or another. Craig came to faith a bit later and spent the first portion of his life as an entrepreneur and a businessman.

What we have in common is a deep desire to be the real thing when it comes to following Jesus and to help others become authentic followers of Jesus as well. Something else we have in common is a genuine love for the Bride of Christ, the Church. With

2. See https://www.spiritual-leadership.org/.

all our brokenness, division, isolation, distractions, and constant challenges, Jesus is still inviting us to participate with him in the transformation of the world. Another thing we share in common is the faith to believe that nothing is impossible for our God. No obstacle we are facing, no challenge that is coming, can stand against what God is doing in the world. Finally, we also have just enough audacity to believe that any of us who are willing can join Jesus in the power of the Holy Spirit to see this world change to the glory of God.

This book is an invitation. Take a deep breath as we begin. Come with us on an adventure into Jesus' Kingdom and imagine yourself as one who can create space for Passionate Spiritual Disciples to thrive and multiply.

Chapter 1

DELIGHTFUL DISCOVERY

The wonderful sensation when discovering the changing sky of a beautiful sunrise or locating what you have been struggling to find can be truly delightful. In our work to build transformative environments we've had front-row seats to people discovering how to live out their callings, delighting in the freedom that comes from a life aligned with glorious purpose.

We have been plugging away for years looking for ways to help people find the joy of working together to create transformative environments, and we have had the privilege of seeing the shining eyes[1] of a person who has just discovered or rediscovered how wonderful being connected to Jesus is. Our work takes us into ministries that would like to become healthier and to overcome some of the patterns of behavior that lock in their existing culture. Needless to say, this can be quite challenging and requires a team of people with deep trust who are willing to learn and risk together. It is a wonderful thing when joy replaces being overwhelmed, when alignment replaces randomness, and when people become motivated into loving action.

---

1. The phrase "shining eyes" comes from Rosamund Stone Zander and Benjamin Zander, *The Art of Possibility: Transforming Professional and Personal Life* (Cambridge, MA: Harvard Business School Press, 2000).

In the last few years, we have had a delightful discovery and believe that we have found simplicity on the other side of complexity.[2] We hope what follows will put in your hands what we have learned.

Adventure Awaits

In the heart of my (Craig's) childhood, adventure called me like a magnet, drawing me into a world of wonder-filled experiences. From crafting leaf boats in puddles to navigating stormy weather, nature became my playground. Vacationing on northern Michigan lakes brought an annual dose of excitement, making me yearn for the thrill of swimming, boating, and skiing.

As adolescence dawned, the allure of waterside views intensified, with reflections doubling the beauty of sunsets and approaching storms. Despite driving my parents to the edge, waiting an hour after meals became a necessary pause between my water escapades.

Growing up, the love for water persisted through life's practicalities, culminating in the acquisition of a small boat. Hours were devoted to navigating the waters, exploring the limits of extreme sports, and plotting how to spend more time on the water. Now in my sixties, I have fully shifted from thrill-seeking adventures to serene moments of cooking in a secluded cove, napping in the warmth of the sun, and playing games with the kids. However, the joy of navigating boats remains a testament to a divine wiring that fills and blesses me.

---

2. The phrase "simplicity on the other side of complexity" comes from Oliver W. Holmes, *Holmes-Pollock Letters: The Correspondence of Mr. Justice Holmes and Sir Frederick Pollock, 1874–1932*, 2nd ed. (Cambridge, MA: The Belknap Press of Harvard University Press, 1961), 109.

Professionally, I have the privilege of navigating communities with a shared mission. This is a fancy way to say I have been leading organizations. I began this part of my life as a response to what I understood to be a calling on my life from God. I was in my twenties and I was relatively new to following Jesus, but I was all in. I was also blessed to not have any idea what I was doing. The arrangement I thought I negotiated with God was simple: I would work hard, and he would need to fill in everything else that was needed to lead an organization. (Yup, it's crazy to think I negotiated with God!)

Over the years I have found that the same basic principles apply regardless of the size of the organization. If you have thousands you are guiding, you need a small group around you to help do this. If you are part of a small group at church, you have to build relationships with people to communicate and work effectively. It is probably obvious, but regardless of whether you are navigating a boat or a small group, the environment you are working in has an enormous impact on how well things go.

In both cases, creating the right environment is essential if you are hoping to thrive and multiply.

> "Creating the right environment is essential if you are hoping to thrive and multiply."

Like navigating a boat, guiding groups unveiled a mix of art and science, demanding practice, discipline, and environmental focus. Just as in boating, predicting and controlling the winds of change in a community is futile; mastery lies in adjusting to fit the unfolding circumstances.

Lessons from a lifetime filled with piloting a boat, safety classes, and tinkering with the mechanics of a boat seemed to be put to the test on a regular basis. One spring day during a routine boat maneuver, a tiny pin in the engine compartment disconnected, leaving an engine stuck in forward on an eighty-foot boat. In that split second, I not only faced the obvious problems related to motion and the consequences of crashing, but I also faced a set of insecurities that I have gathered about myself. Had this event occurred in open waters, I would have had time to seek council, explore options, try a few experiments, and so on. However, since we were in a tight place, I only had ten seconds to analyze, decide, and act. And so the analysis began:

- Why aren't the controls responding?
- Am I having a stroke?
- Are we really stuck in forward?
- How much is this going to cost?
- Should I say something to the crew about the imminent crash?
- Did I just poop my pants?

These are just the ones I remember. The human brain is really amazing, and there were likely many other thoughts. But you get the idea. I reached up and turned the keys off, eliminating any chance that I could use the engines to slow us down, but this also stopped the acceleration. The boat narrowly slid between rocks that would have sunk the boat, and then it crashed onto shore.

Fortunately, the crew and boat were okay. This moment had come in the midst of a normal routine, created an adaptive challenge, then played out based on a set of practiced values and behaviors.

Countless times, the discomfort of losing control happens in our lives. It happens to the young and old, the professionals and the rookies. It happens whether we want it to or not. The question becomes: Will we let the unknown define us, or will we embrace each experience and allow the experience to contribute to our learning? Ideally, we see these experiences where we lack control as the steps to mastery of our values and growth of our community. I am fortunate to lead a life surrounded by a close-knit circle of family and friends. We share a bond that holds immense value in our relationships and going through life together. On the day the boat collided with the shore, some of these friends made up the crew, and they promptly aided me in navigating this unexpected challenge.

Our established community was pivotal in determining the course of events. We swiftly assessed our situation, questioning if we were sinking, if the captain (myself) had lost his mind, and if external forces like the wind could exacerbate the situation. We quickly ruled out sinking but acknowledged the potential impact of the wind.

Agreeing that stabilizing the boat was our top priority, we took immediate action. We ran ropes to secure the boat, preventing the wind from worsening the scenario. Once it was stable, we focused on investigating the cause of the crash. We located a connector pin that had come loose and failed, causing the boat to be stuck in forward drive. By replacing the pin correctly, the boat was restored to working order.

Crucially, our community had worked together on this adaptive challenge; no one tied me to a chair or shone lights into my eyes. We were able to stay focused on the problems at hand and restore our environment to a healthy state. We were able to adjust in the moment and respond appropriately.

With the crisis resolved, laughter and gratitude followed. This shared experience became another cornerstone of our foundation, reinforcing the resilience of our relationships. Spending ample time together and navigating challenges has cultivated trust that transcends difficulties. Over the years this community has navigated much more difficult situations and been a place where transformation can and does happen.

This same pattern plays out in groups of people wherever they form, including ministries, business, sports, and the arts. Anytime a group of people are willing to journey together, they are actively trying to accomplish something, and they value healthy relationships, the potential for a thriving environment exists.

> Two things are important to mention. The first is that whether you are part of a thriving environment or not, life has difficult things coming your way. There is no evidence to support that a certain type of people is able to miss out on the difficulties of life. So being part of a thriving environment doesn't exclude you from really difficult situations. However, being part of a thriving community is way better when things are hard.
>
> The second thing that is important to mention is that anyone can facilitate the starting and managing of a thriving environment. Just like the above statement, there is no evidence that more education, credentials, wealth, or anything else gives you an advantage for creating a thriving environment.

How Did We Get Here?
Working Backward to the Root Cause

What do you imagine as the ultimate fruit of the ministry of the church in the world? We have an assumption that you are longing for *impact* in the world today that looks like the Kingdom of God on earth. In other words, you imagine the realities of heaven becoming the realities of earth right where you live, work, and play.

You dream of seeing and experiencing the Gospels and the book of Acts all over again in our twenty-first-century world.

This is precisely what we pray for each time we cry out for the Lord's Kingdom to come and his will to be done. Do we believe it is possible? It is!

In order to see this, we will most certainly need a miraculous move of God in our day. In fact, we need the kind of move of God that leads to us becoming *thriving, resilient,* and *generative.*

Has God forgotten to move? Is God's arm too short to save? Certainly not. Then what are we missing?

If only God can bring this kind of transformation, participating with God to experience transformation will require a certain kind of *spiritual leaders* who embody a particular posture and practices. And given the complexities of the challenges we are facing today, we actually need *teams of spiritual leaders* who are Leading Together through the valleys and toward the vision of Kingdom impact in the world.

Most of our churches, though, are not *thriving, resilient,* and *generative,* and we often lack the kind of *spiritual leaders* who love and lead like Jesus and by the Spirit are a witness in this broken world. In order to grow more passionate spiritual leaders who can lead to greater thriving in our churches, we must first have *passionate spiritual disciples.*

When we boil it all down, the root cause for the lack of impact and fruitfulness of the church is a shortage of authentic disciples of Jesus.

> "The root cause for the lack of impact and fruitfulness of the church is a shortage of authentic disciples of Jesus."

Here Is Some Evidence!

While the picture of impact and Kingdom fruitfulness may be in our minds at times, much of our church activity is not connected to that picture. Many of our churches may even have vision statements that point toward these things and mission statements that are focused on making disciples. In our ministry settings, though, we are often working on things that have little to no connection with people actually becoming authentic followers of Jesus. Our focus is often more on the programs we run and the events we host, and our metrics are about the numbers of people in those programs and events and the amount of money we collect.

As a point of reference, think of your typical children's ministry in a church. A ton of time is spent on an ongoing basis just trying to recruit volunteers to serve in various capacities. Many children's ministry leaders feel overwhelmed, frustrated by this constant need for volunteers, and that they have to resort to any and every form of persuasion, coercion, and even manipulation in order to get people to help.

What if the church was full of authentic disciples of Jesus? Would the reality be different enough that recruiting would be different? In churches with true disciples of Jesus, people are serving regularly based on their passions and giftedness as an organic part of their discipleship. If this is true, recruiting is about connecting called and gifted disciples to serve where they are most passionate. Equipping disciples leads to mobilized disciples.

How about another example? Many churches have regular stewardship campaigns to meet the current or future needs of the church or the community. Pastors and church leaders often feel awkward asking for money even for worthy causes. Average giving by church attendees is quite low.[3] As a result, and not unlike our children's ministry example, compelling people to give their money often requires charisma, persuasion, and even manipulation. What would be different, though, if the stewardship *ask* was given to real followers of Jesus rather than mere church attendees? Like service, giving is an organic and joy-filled part of the life of a true disciple.

Take a minute and think about all the things that are most frustrating about church and ministry. Think of all the things that churches are doing to compensate for not having enough disciples. How much of our time is spent on things that are only necessary because we do not have the kind of disciples we need?

> "Think of all the things that churches are doing to compensate for not having enough disciples."

An Important Caveat and Invitation

It is important to name here that most of our current church activities and programs have good intentions behind them. In fact, most of those activities and programs were likely launched as an attempt to more effectively help people grow as disciples. They may have even seen that kind of fruitfulness at some point in time. We have no desire to criticize something that God has used in the past to help people relate to God and others and to grow in their faith.

Our invitation here is to step back from everything you currently do and simply ask if you are seeing what you long to see.

---

3. Barna Group, "What Is a Tithe? New Data on Perceptions of the 10 Percent," Barna Group, September 7, 2022, https://www.barna.com/research/what-is-a-tithe/.

Imagine for a moment that you can get to a mountain ridge and look down into the valley on all you and your church have experienced in the past, are experiencing in the present, and are longing for in the future. If your current trajectory is not leading you toward the future impact and fruitfulness that you know God is calling you to, what might you do differently?

We have no desire to displace any program or activity you are doing. In fact, the Lord may be calling you to a renewal of something that has brought impact for you. What we are inviting you to is not about new programs but instead about a shift in culture and way of being that is entirely focused on becoming authentic followers of Jesus. Our hope in the pages that follow is to paint a picture of creating a culture of *passionate spiritual disciples.*

What if God is inviting you now into a new adventure filled with the wonder and joy of childlike faith? Perhaps you feel like the engine is stuck in forward as if you are trapped doing the same things you have always done with no hope of things changing. What if it is time for you to turn that engine off to assess your current situation and imagine with Spirit-filled eyes what more intentional focus and impact could be?

I (Bryan) have a friend who worked his entire career as a pastor, more than forty years, and he had announced his retirement. His current role was more administrative for his denomination after serving as the senior pastor of several churches for decades before that. He was looking forward to some rest and travel with his wife in retirement, but he had become unsettled about his decision to retire. I had the great honor of being in a coaching conversation with him where he named that he didn't think he could retire. When I asked him why, he simply said, "Because I haven't seen *it* yet."

What is *it?* He went on to say that what he hadn't seen yet was the kind of deep transformation in the lives of ordinary people that God had called him to. What he had seen and even led was a ton of church meetings, sermons, church programs, and the like. What he was still dreaming of was seeing people become authentic disciples of Jesus who by their very lives, in word and deed, were helping others become followers of Jesus as well and participating in Jesus' Kingdom on earth.

What was incomplete in his life was that he knew God had placed him on the planet with a clear sense of purpose and passion for this calling to see people truly follow Jesus, and to that point he'd spent his life doing church stuff instead of truly living for this passion and calling.

I'm excited to say that my friend un-retired and found himself helping lead a church that was intentional and focused on guiding people to become sold out, accountable, disciple-making followers of Jesus. After multiple decades of just leading a church, he became who God had called him to be and saw the kind of transformation he longed to see.

The concept of redirecting the focus of churches toward transformative environments aligns with fostering spiritual growth and sanctification, moving beyond merely baptizing new members and running church programs. It encourages a profound commitment to Jesus' teachings and their practical application.

The foundation for this transformative environment lies in making it commonplace for disciples to discuss their deeper sense of purpose and calling as an integral part of their primary work within and outside the local church. Rather than hoping for assistance with everything, disciples take responsibility and consider the local church as a resource they carry into their daily lives.

Initiating conversations about *spiritual, relational,* and *missional* health becomes less daunting when certain beliefs are embraced. Acknowledging oneself as a participant rather than an expert is crucial. The understanding that people appreciate genuine listeners facilitates open dialogue in which individuals feel safe to share their stories, strengths, and weaknesses.

The immense potential of guiding discussions about *spiritual, relational,* and *missional* health becomes evident. Individuals discovering and pursuing their purpose and calling desire spiritual formation and yearn for healthy relationships to foster personal growth.

A countercultural but essential concept emerges—identifying the most important ministry. This is not merely serving at church; it's about discerning and pursuing the unique calling that God has designed for each person. This perspective challenges conventional norms, emphasizing the significance of aligning with God's purpose rather than conforming to traditional expectations.

In the chapters that follow, we want to take you on a journey of delightful discovery that helps you identify what a passionate spiritual disciple is, provides you with some practical steps for how to be this kind of disciple and invite others around you to do so as well, and which paints a picture of how creating the right kinds of environments can be a catalyst for the thriving and multiplication of passionate spiritual disciples. The following figure depicts where we are headed in this book.

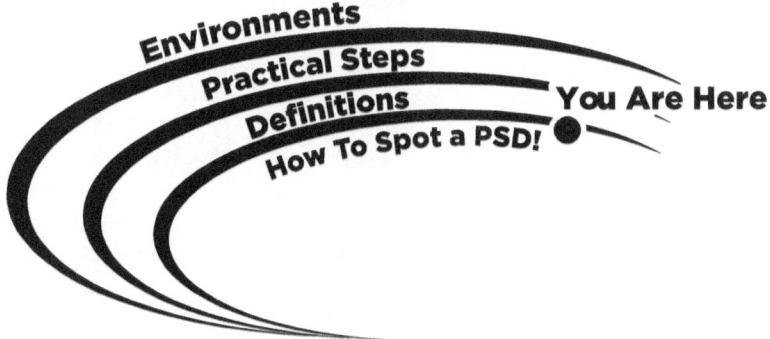

Questions for Personal Reflection and Group Discussion

1. Think of a time in your life when you have had a "delightful discovery." What made that delightful?

2. Have you ever considered the power of the environments or spaces you create? In your experience, what makes for a thriving environment?

3. As you read this chapter, what challenged you most?

4. As you reflect on what you are reading, what insights connect with you best?

Chapter 2

IDENTIFYING WHAT A PASSIONATE SPIRITUAL DISCIPLE IS

We know that God has chosen disciples of Jesus to effect change in the world. We envision followers of Jesus finding joy in the adventure of growing into the image of Christ as they are also constantly growing in their ability to lean on God's Spirit to help navigate all of life. While there are many resources on how to discover God's calling on your life, and the ideas of going deep into the center of God's love have been written about for centuries, many of us feel that our contributions are not producing sufficient fruit. As we watch the culture spiral away from church and we see the effects of isolation growing, the question becomes, Is there something in this moment that would be more fruitful? We are proposing a new target: the creation of environments where Passionate Spiritual Disciples thrive and multiply.

Imagine for a moment what it would have been like to be in Thomas Edison's shoes. As an inventor and businessman, Edison was unsatisfied with his current context and curious about what was possible. He is best known for inventing early versions of the electric light bulb; however, he is also responsible for inventing the phonograph and the motion picture camera. What we were unaware of until recently is that Edison was one of the first inventors to apply teamwork to the process of invention. He was not only an inventor himself, he created the environment for invention and experimentation. Imagine him surrounding himself with people who shared his passion, and together they found new solutions to otherwise impossible challenges.[1]

As we pursue describing what a disciple is and how to cultivate environments for disciples of Jesus to thrive and multiply, we encourage you to come at this like an inventor or adventurer. If God is the Creator and we are made in God's image, what kind of environments or spaces might God want to create in and through us?

PSD Definition

As we describe what a true follower of Jesus is like, we use the language of a Passionate Spiritual Disciple. What does that mean? A Passionate Spiritual Disciple (PSD) is *an authentic follower of Jesus as Lord, filled with and embodying the Spirit's fruit.*

Before walking through this definition of a Passionate Spiritual Disciple, we have to be clear as to what a disciple is. How would you describe or define what a disciple is?

When my (Bryan's) oldest son was seven years old, he and I began a journey of discovery together about what a disciple is. We were discussing some of Greg Ogden's work in *Discipleship Essentials.*[2] I wanted to make sure these conversations were sticking for my son, so I asked him to describe a disciple in his own words. His response went something like this: "Well, Dad, it's kind of

---

1. "Thomas Edison," last modified May 22, 2024, https://en.wikipedia.org/wiki/Thomas_Edison.
2. Greg Ogden, *Discipleship Essentials: A Guide to Building Your Life in Christ* (Downers Grove, IL: InterVarsity Press, 2019).

like Star Wars. You know how Luke Skywalker is being trained by Obi-Wan Kenobi? Luke is his apprentice. And the whole point is for the apprentice to become like the master."

I'll never forget this conversation. At seven years old, he captured the essence of what it means to be a disciple. A disciple is indeed an apprentice, a follower, a learner. And the whole point is to become like our Master, Jesus.

So what makes a disciple a Passionate Spiritual Disciple? We intentionally use *spiritual* language to emphasize that we are only true disciples of Jesus if we are empowered by the Holy Spirit. In fact, it is impossible for us to be true disciples of Jesus without the Spirit drawing us, growing us, and empowering us. We find that as the Spirit does this work in us, we grow more and more *passionate* about following Jesus and helping others to do so as well. One definition of *passion* is "a strong liking or desire for or devotion to some activity, object, or concept."[3] This language of desire and devotion is critical. Some link passion with mere exuberance or excitement in a way that would only fit with a certain type of outgoing personality. As we are discussing passion, though, it can show up in very quiet as well as very energetic ways. Passion doesn't have a volume setting. True disciples are being continually shaped by the Holy Spirit and are growing more and more passionate about Jesus and his Kingdom.

> "A Passionate Spiritual Disciple (PSD) is an authentic follower of Jesus as Lord, filled with and embodying the Spirit's fruit."

---

3. *Merriam-Webster Dictionary*, s.v. "passion," accessed May 29, 2024, https://www.merriam-webster.com/dictionary/passion.

Authentic Follower

This all leads to our definition of a Passionate Spiritual Disciple: *an authentic follower of Jesus as Lord, filled with and embodying the Spirit's fruit.* First off, an *authentic follower* of Jesus is not merely a churchgoer or someone who has prayed a prayer at an altar. In order to be an actual disciple there has to be a true and ongoing encounter with Jesus that results in actually following Jesus and becoming more like him as his apprentice.

Let's break down this language of "true" and "ongoing." Have you had a true encounter with Jesus? I (Bryan) had one of the most joyful and exciting conversations recently. For several years I have been working with an organizational leader who works for a Christian nonprofit organization. She grew up Catholic and seems to have believed generally in God. What she has discovered over the past few months is that she had never pursued or understood a real relationship with Jesus. I noticed something different in her a couple of months ago and was thrilled to hear her describe that she has given her life to Jesus. For the first time this has become a personal and authentic encounter with Jesus. Once a religious observer, she has now become an actual follower of Jesus.

The next question is whether your encounter with Jesus is "ongoing." We have been invited by Jesus to "abide in me as I abide in you" (John 15:4). This abiding is initiated by Jesus himself. His very presence is within us if we are in Christ. Our abiding in Jesus is a response to his continual abiding in us. The invitation, though, is not to come to Jesus merely when we need him but instead to live continually in Jesus' presence. Am I abiding in Jesus as he abides in me? This is ongoing encounter.

Jesus as Lord

A Passionate Spiritual Disciple follows *Jesus as Lord.* In other words, Jesus is not only our Savior, but he is also our leader and master. In his book *The Forgotten Ways*, Alan Hirsch takes a deep look at the early church and the Chinese underground church as the two greatest movements in church history.[4] He describes six dynamics of these powerful and world-changing movements. The central dynamic of these movements is the confession that Jesus is Lord. Jesus is the center! We are a Jesus movement.

The key question for each of us is whether Jesus really is Lord—that is, whether our greatest adoration, priorities, and motivations are centered in Jesus. One of our heroes in the faith, the late Robert Mulholland, wrote a remarkable book about spiritual formation titled *Invitation to a Journey.* In it, he defines spiritual formation as "a process of being conformed to the image of Christ for the sake of others."[5] Mulholland describes that our whole life must become consecrated to Jesus whereby we continually say yes to God at each point of our unlikeness to him. Mulholland wrote, "The points of unlikeness to Christ are areas of our life where we are lord and not Christ."[6]

Filled

As we empty ourselves to God, we are *filled* with the Spirit, who is constantly transforming us to become more like Jesus. Many of us are *filled* with many things that get in the way of what the

---

4. Alan Hirsch, *The Forgotten Ways: Reactivating Apostolic Movements* (Grand Rapids, MI: Brazos Press, 2016).
5. M. Robert Mulholland Jr., *Invitation to a Journey: A Road Map for Spiritual Formation* (Grand Rapids, MI: InterVarsity Press, 1993), 12.
6. Mulholland, 41–42.

Spirit wants in and through us. For instance, some of us are consumed with so many things that we lack the space and capacity in our lives to be focused on being true followers of Jesus. Our calendars are full beyond our margins, and even our leisure time is full of things that do not leave room. Many of our churches are full of programs and events that are not primarily focused on forming disciples. Passionate Spiritual Disciples are on a continuing journey to let go of the noise of a hurried life and give the Spirit room—to create space for God.[7] Only an empty vessel can be truly *filled.*

Mulholland reminds us that we are not conforming ourselves to Christ but instead being conformed.[8] This requires us to let go of control and trust the Lord. The apostle Paul said, "Now the Lord is the Spirit, and where the Spirit of the Lord is, there is freedom. And we all, who with unveiled faces contemplate the Lord's glory, are being transformed into his image with ever-increasing glory, which comes from the Lord, who is the Spirit" (2 Corinthians 3:17–18 NIV). It is the Spirit who is filling and working in us so that we are being transformed to become more and more like our Master, Jesus.

Being filled and formed by the Spirit "is the great reversal: from being the subject who controls all things to being a person who is shaped by the presence, purpose, and power of God in all things."[9] We are reminded "that it is God, not we ourselves, who is the source of the transformation of our being into wholeness in the image of Christ. Our part is to offer ourselves to God in ways

---

7. For more on this subject, see John Mark Comer, *The Ruthless Elimination of Hurry: How to Stay Emotionally Healthy and Spiritually Alive in the Chaos of the Modern World* (Colorado Springs: WaterBrook, 2019).
8. Mulholland, *Invitation to a Journey*, 25–32.
9. Mulholland, 27.

that enable God to do that transforming work of grace."[10] Our willingness to yield to God creates space for the Spirit to fill us and form us into Christ's image.

Embodying the Spirit's Fruit

As the Spirit fills us, we *embody the Spirit's fruit* through our lives. The apostle Paul makes it clear that the fruit of the Spirit is love, joy, peace, patience, kindness, goodness, faithfulness, gentleness, and self-control (see Galatians 5:22–23). These are a natural (or supernatural) consequence of truly abiding in Jesus and being filled and formed by the Spirit. These fruit are relational in nature and represent the very character of God that the Spirit is forming in us for the sake of others.

Mulholland encourages us to reflect on what the image of Christ really is: "It is the image of One who gave himself totally, completely, absolutely, unconditionally for others."[11] And N. T. Wright reminds us that true followers of Jesus take on the very virtues of Jesus over time as the Spirit works in us by grace.[12] In other words, we embody the character of Jesus and the fruit of the Spirit in real ways to the glory of God.

And so a Passionate Spiritual Disciple is *an authentic follower of Jesus as Lord, filled with and embodying the Spirit's fruit.* Before imagining how we might create the environments and spaces for others to become Passionate Spiritual Disciples, I have to ask myself if I am one. How would I know?

---

10.   Mulholland, 30.
11.   Mulholland, 41.
12.   N. T. Wright, *After You Believe: The Forgotten Role of Virtue in the Christian Life* (New York: HarperOne, 2010).

PSD Fruit: Growing in Spiritual, Relational, and Missional Health

What is the fruit of being a Passionate Spiritual Disciple? A Passionate Spiritual Disciple is *growing in spiritual, relational, and missional health.*

A true disciple of Jesus is always growing. As we mentioned previously, this growth is guided and empowered by the Holy Spirit to the glory of God. In church circles, it is not uncommon for people to discuss the importance of spiritual growth, which is indeed a critical aspect of growth in our lives as followers of Jesus. Along with this, though, it is important to include growing in both relational and missional ways that imitate Jesus. These three areas of growth are all integrated and are initiated and empowered by the Holy Spirit.

> "A Passionate Spiritual Disciple is growing in spiritual, relational, and missional health."

Spiritual Growth

How does a person grow spiritually to become more like Jesus? There are many different means by which a person can grow spiritually. It is important to remember that these are a *means* and not the end. The aim of being formed spiritually, as Mulholland states, is to be conformed to the image of Christ for the sake of others.[13] The *means of grace*, also referred to as spiritual practices, habits, or disciplines, are meant to put us into a posture of readiness for the Holy Spirit to do the sanctifying work of conforming

---

13. Mulholland, *Invitation to a Journey.*

us to become more like Jesus. Prayer, worship, diving deep into Scripture, fasting, fellowship with other believers, sharing our faith, solitude, and other such spiritual practices put us in the environment where God can deeply commune with us and work in and through us.

I (Bryan) was raised in a Christian home with parents who were very dedicated to Jesus and in a church deeply committed to forming people to become like Jesus. Somehow in that environment, though, I held a perspective that being religiously disciplined was the way to please God. While I knew that I was only saved by grace, I practiced my faith as if everything else depended on me.

Now, it is important to state here that no one taught me this. In fact, I was likely taught better theology than this. Something about my own personality (and perhaps birth order—I am a firstborn) combined with the particular environment in which I was raised contributed to this dysfunctional view. I have discovered through interacting with many people throughout my life, though, that I am not the only one with this perspective.

What this perspective led to was feeling good about myself when I was doing the right things and feeling shame and self-pity when I was not. Notice how neither of these turned out to conform me to become more like Jesus.

Being formed spiritually in a way that leads to spiritual health is always a response to God's goodness, faithfulness, holiness, and love. According to the Scripture, we are not made righteous by what we do, but instead righteousness is credited to us by virtue of what Christ has done for us through the cross and his resurrection as we believe and place our full trust in Christ (Genesis 15:6;

2 Corinthians 5:14–21). In response to Christ's outrageous love for us, we are invited to abide in him as he abides in us (John 15:1–11).

What if we are already fully accepted by God and completely loved by the Father no matter what we do or don't do? Remember Jesus received his affirmation from the Father as one who was beloved and pleasing before any public act of ministry (Matthew 3:16–17). You are God's beloved and are pleasing to God simply by being his son or daughter. Do you believe this?[14]

> "What if we are already fully accepted by God and completely loved by the Father no matter what we do or don't do?"

I think about my own four children and my love for them. I cannot imagine a scenario that would cause my love for them to fade. It certainly is not a perfect love, but I know it isn't based on their actions. In light of this, I have a simple practice that I have done with each of them since they were little. I tell them that I love them and I am proud of them. Then I ask, "Why am I most proud of you?" They simply respond, "Because I am your son or daughter."

I am reminded here of Jesus' words: "If you then, though you are evil, know how to give good gifts to your children, how much more will your Father in heaven give the Holy Spirit to those who ask him!" (Luke 11:13 NIV).

This is where the next invitation to invention and adventure takes place. Remember our opening anchor story about the childhood wonder-filled experiences of being on the water. What if walking with Jesus is supposed to be filled with that same kind of wonder, adventure, and joy? What if rather than viewing God

---

14. For more on understanding and living as beloved children of God, see Wes Olds, *Confronting the Thief Within: How I Quit Earning God's Love and Embraced My Real Identity* (Plano, TX: Invite Press, 2023).

as disappointed and distant, we could begin seeing God as eager to commune and already near? Jesus is inviting you to abide with him as he is already abiding with you. He is inviting you to abide in his love just as he is abiding in the Father's love. He is inviting you to experience his complete joy. Following Jesus through the lens of wonder, adventure, and joy does not mean that everything in life will be easy or fun. In fact, living with this perspective can and does coexist with walking through lament, grief, and pain—just as we discussed the idea that passion, joy, and wonder do not have to look like exuberance. They can and do show up in stillness and quiet as well. Abiding in the joy of Jesus in this way will naturally lead to the fruit of growth in you (see John 15:1–11).

> "What if walking with Jesus is supposed to be filled with wonder, adventure, and joy?"

How can you create space every day in which you can become more like Jesus? If you can begin to approach your walk with Jesus in this way, what might shift in your approach to practicing the means of grace? What if these practices, like prayer, worship, reading Scripture, and fasting, are simply a way to create the environment for you to abide intimately with Jesus in response to his love and invitation? What if every day is another opportunity to say yes to God in any and all places that are unlike Jesus? What if we can trust the Holy Spirit to continually do the work of growing and forming us into Christ's image as we simply empty ourselves and yield to him?

Take a moment now and *ask the Holy Spirit to show you one way that you can abide more deeply in Christ Jesus*. Start with that one thing, and keep asking and responding to that question every week.

Relational Growth

How does a person grow relationally to become more like Jesus? Mulholland makes it clear that we are conformed to the image of Christ *for the sake of others.* This means that we are not formed merely for our own good but also (and perhaps primarily) for the good of others. There are always relational consequences to our own spiritual formation. Jesus named for us that his greatest commandment is that we love God with our all and love others as we love ourselves (see Matthew 22:37–40). The apostle John reminded us that we cannot claim to love God if we do not also love our brother and sister (see 1 John 4:19–21).

In connection to this, Mulholland states,

> If you want a good litmus test of your spiritual growth, simply examine the nature and quality of your relationships with others. Are you more loving, more compassionate, more patient, more understanding, more caring, more giving, more forgiving than you were a year ago? If you cannot answer these kinds of questions in the affirmative and, especially, if others cannot answer them in the affirmative about you, then you need to examine carefully the nature of your spiritual life and growth.[15]

As we discussed previously, the fruit of the Spirit (love, joy, peace, patience, kindness, goodness, faithfulness, gentleness, and self-control) is what the Holy Spirit brings in and through us as we are formed into the image of Christ. These are not things we can manufacture on our own. Notice the relational dynamic of each of these fruit. These fruit are not for us to show off, and while we are personally blessed by experiencing these things, the fruits

---

15. Mulholland, 42.

are primarily *for the sake of others.* This is the very nature of Jesus and of God, to be constantly and selflessly focused on another.

Picture someone you know who always reminds you of Jesus. I think of my friend Scott, who recently traveled a long way to bring me a gift for my son. Then just today I received an email from him that was purely meant to encourage me to fully live into who God made me to be. When I observe his life, he exhibits the fruit of the Spirit. He loves and brings joy and peace to others in sacrificial ways that take him out of what is easy and comfortable. He creates environments for people to become Passionate Spiritual Disciples.

> "And here again is an invitation to adventure and wonder. What would it be like to truly experience and share the love, joy, peace, patience, kindness, goodness, faithfulness, gentleness, and self-control of Jesus?"

And here again is an invitation to adventure and wonder. What would it be like to truly experience and share the love, joy, peace, patience, kindness, goodness, faithfulness, gentleness, and self-control of Jesus? How can you create environments to express these fruit as a blessing for others? What if you began to see yourself first and foremost as God's beloved child and an agent of God's love to others? How might you be a joy-giver and peacemaker for those who are hopeless and broken?

Take a moment now and **ask the Lord to show you one relationship where you can bear the Holy Spirit's fruit.** Start with that one thing, and keep asking and responding to that question every week.

Missional Growth

How does a person grow missionally to become more like Jesus? Our growth spiritually and relationally to become more like Jesus naturally moves us toward joining with Jesus in mission. Jesus invites us, like he did his first disciples, into his very mission and ministry: "Then Jesus came to them and said, 'All authority in heaven and on earth has been given to me. Therefore go and make disciples of all nations, baptizing them in the name of the Father and of the Son and of the Holy Spirit, and teaching them to obey everything I have commanded you. And surely I am with you always, to the very end of the age'" (Matthew 28:18–20 NIV).

Notice that this is not our mission but Jesus' mission. We have been invited into it and reminded that we do not do this alone. It is easy to get the notion that we are doing work for God, but Jesus makes it clear that he is always with us. We are joining Jesus in what he is already doing in the world.[16]

In concert with this invitation from Jesus, the apostle Paul reminded us that it is Christ's love that compels us and we've been given the very ministry of Jesus. God is the one transforming people, relationships, systems, and society, yet we have the great privilege of being Christ's ambassadors in the world (see 2 Corinthians 5:14–21).

The prophet Micah succinctly painted the picture of what is good and what the Lord requires of us: "To act justly and to love mercy and to walk humbly with your God" (Micah 6:8 NIV). Justice, mercy, and humility are all attributes of our God of love, and

---

16. For more on this subject, see Skye Jathani, *With: Reimagining the Way You Relate to God* (Nashville: Thomas Nelson, 2001).

empowered by the Spirit we are the ambassadors of this love in God's world.

Over the centuries people have been doing mission with Jesus, and often their stories don't translate well into our lives. I mean, really? Swallowed by a fish, led an army, crawled up to the king on hands and knees, poured oil on Jesus, got out of a boat and walked on the water? We read these stories and often forget how they begin. *So I was fishing, and Jesus said that I was heading in the right direction but needed to adjust to fishing for people* (Peter). *I was using my ability with numbers and details, and I needed to adjust and use these abilities in a team of disciples* (Matthew). God created us and within our being made us unique, special, and talented. Because we are all created in the image of God, the question becomes, How do I describe my unique contribution? Our mission or our calling will not work without Jesus, but we do need to pay attention to the fact that God, in his infinite wisdom, made us all different. A Passionate Spiritual Disciple is someone who is learning and growing with Jesus in their uniqueness. When we talk about having a calling or deeper sense of purpose, this is what we mean.

I (Bryan) have a dear friend and mentor with a profound, unique, but common call story. He grew up with little connection to God or church until a girl invited him to consider faith as a young adult. Self-admittedly, his pursuit of God began simply because of the girl. (She later became his wife, but only after he committed his life to Jesus.) He eventually gave his life to Christ and even had profound experiences with the Lord and some key friends in a small group.

He had never considered, though, that he could have a unique calling. He was faithful in church and even served on committees, passed out bulletins, and pressed play on the tape to accompany his wife's singing. He took his faith seriously, but it didn't really apply to most of his Monday-through-Saturday life.

In his day job, he was an entrepreneur who was constantly creating new things and, frankly, changing the world. He built multiple businesses, interacting with local, state, and federal governments in ways that improved their service and impact.

For someone this on the go, church was a bit slow and at times boring. His leadership prowess and capacity often made him intimidating to pastors and church staff. It was normal to be asked to serve in places that didn't match his gifts. Because he had never been to seminary and didn't feel he knew his Bible well enough, he assumed this was his proper place in the church as "just a layperson."

Eventually, he had a pastor with the courage to invite him and another friend into a mutual and collaborative relationship. The pastor mentored the two laymen in spiritual growth, but the two laymen mentored the pastor in leadership development. A few years later, yet another pastor invited these same two men into a handpicked, small group of other women and men, who underwent a formation process that lasted several years.

These experiences brought with them the invitation for my friend to consider that God could be calling him to something unique—that there might be a deeper purpose for his life. He and the other layman began considering what their postretirement life would look like and how they might create something that could serve church leaders. At this time, he was in the early stages of launching yet another company when the Nasdaq crashed and investors pulled out. That crash gave him room to consider stepping into a calling to walk alongside church leaders to grow spiritually, relationally, and missionally. It was and is a calling that requires constant prayer, dependence on God, collaboration with others, and consistent stepping out into the unknown.

This is actually Craig's story, and it led to the launch of SLI (Spiritual Leadership, Inc.). In our work coaching leaders and churches over the past couple decades, we have seen countless people grow and multiply as Passionate Spiritual Disciples. This calling is uniquely suited for Craig and provides him continual opportunities to go on joy-filled, exciting, and risk-taking adventures.

I (Bryan) began this story by describing it as profound, unique, but common. This is what I find to be true of every call story. God works in such profound ways and invites us each into something that is uniquely tailored to how he has made us and who he is inviting us to become. This demonstrates God's deeply personal love for each of us as his children and image bearers. Yet because this is true for each one of us, this story is also common. What I mean by this is that none of us is more special than any other. Craig's call is powerful, as is mine, as is yours. It is easy to assume that there is an elite form of being a Christian and then everyone else is "normal." Yet the same Spirit who raised Christ from the dead lives in you and in me (Romans 8:11), just like the Spirit lived in the apostle Paul and whomever your hero of the faith is.

In this section, we have described the importance and necessity of every disciple pursuing their calling. This is language that some would reserve only for professional clergy, but we use this language to describe the unique sense of purpose that God brings to every follower of Jesus. All are called. All are gifted. All are empowered.

First and foremost, we are all called to follow Jesus. This calling is the same for each of us and is the essence of what it means to be a disciple. Jesus is calling us to restored relationship with God, and he has made the way for that restoration possible. This is the true and ongoing encounter and abiding with Jesus we described earlier in this chapter.

Each follower of Jesus, though, also has a secondary calling or deep sense of purpose that is connected to that first call. Calling, in this secondary way, is generally defined as "a strong inner impulse toward a particular course of action especially when accompanied by conviction of divine influence."[17]

For some, this secondary calling becomes linked to vocation in some way where people make at least part of their living serving and helping others. This can be true of teachers, aid workers, community developers, pastors, healthcare workers, missionaries, and coaches, to name a few. For many others, though, this calling may be indirectly tied to their vocation by the way they live and serve others in their work environment, home, or community.

You may have never considered yourself as having a calling. In fact, many Christians do not consciously live with a deeper sense of purpose. This is why creating environments to foster this is so important. Or perhaps you do have a clear sense of calling but do not feel as if your life is deeply connected to that call. The key here is to acknowledge that Jesus is indeed calling you to follow him and to invite others to do the same both in how you live and by what you say.

For us, there is a deep connection between passion and calling, and all of this relates to our missional health following Jesus.

---

17. *Merriam-Webster Dictionary*, s.v. "calling," accessed May 29, 2024, https://www.merriam-webster.com/dictionary/calling.

Earlier in this chapter we described how authentic disciples are both passionate and spiritual. Using spiritual language acknowledges that we can only be authentic disciples if we are guided, filled, formed, and empowered by the Holy Spirit. In fact, even our relational and missional health is deeply spiritual. As the apostle Paul put it, "Since we live by the Spirit, let us keep in step with the Spirit" (Galatians 5:25 NIV). As we abide in Jesus and keep in step with the Spirit, our passions are aligned and transformed by the Spirit.[18]

What are you passionate about? Does living into that passion give you a sense of purpose and belonging? How might what you are most passionate about be connected to your calling? How might you create environments around that passion that would help you become more fully who God made you to be as a PSD and invite others to do the same?

> "What are you passionate about? Does living into that passion give you a sense of purpose and belonging? How might what you are most passionate about be connected to your calling?"

As I (Bryan) write this I am sitting under a tree by the water. I imagine Jesus inviting us away from the safety and security of the shore and out into the boat on the water with him, inviting us to let go of being a spectator to what he is doing to instead become an active participant. He is the captain this time, but we have a glorious part to play in what he is doing. He is making all things new and setting all things right, and we get to be on his team. As in our story in chapter 1, there will certainly be challenges and

---

18.   For more on the subject of calling, see Os Guinness, *The Call: Finding and Fulfilling the Central Purpose of Your Life* (Nashville: Thomas Nelson, 1998).

situations where things do not go as we planned or imagined. He is always there, though. We are never alone.

Jesus said, "Anyone who welcomes you welcomes me, and anyone who welcomes me welcomes the one who sent me" (Matthew 10:40 NIV). Everywhere you go, Jesus goes with you. Whenever you show up in a situation, people get Jesus and the Father who sent Jesus.

> "Whenever you show up in a situation,
> people get Jesus."

So here again is an invitation to join Jesus on an adventure with wonder, joy, and anticipation. What if we can live our lives as actual ambassadors of Jesus? What if we lived with the continual awareness that wherever we show up, that is an environment for people to encounter Jesus? What if we could realize that we are not only invited into mission with Jesus, but we have the privilege of inviting others into that mission with Jesus as well?

Take a moment now and **ask the Holy Spirit to show you one way that you can join Jesus in mission.** Start with that one thing, and keep asking and responding to that question every week.

How Can You Tell If Someone Is a PSD?

How do you know when you have a Passionate Spiritual Disciple? In other words, what are the key indicators that demonstrate growth in people becoming Passionate Spiritual Disciples?

When you go to the doctor, they always assess the same few things as indicators of health or warning signs of something unhealthy. These are called *vital signs*. In the case of our physical health, two examples are our temperature and blood pressure. There are standards of health in these two categories that we are all familiar with (temperature at 98.6 degrees Fahrenheit, blood pressure at 120/80), but if we are significantly off of these standards, either high or low, this is a warning sign that points to something unhealthy.

A number of years ago, I (Bryan) was diagnosed with high blood pressure. At several check-ups in a row, my doctor had been tracking my blood pressure, and it was consistently high. I have a history of high blood pressure in my family, so this was not a surprise. I explained to the doctor that I preferred not to go on blood pressure medicines, at least not yet, and asked for his recommendation. He suggested a strict low-sodium diet and daily exercise, and he made me a follow-up appointment in a month. After following his recommendation, we were both pleased to see that my blood pressure had improved, and I was able to stay off of medication.

I mention this personal story because of what the doctor said next. He looked me in the eyes and said to me, "You are the first patient who has ever followed my advice that strictly." What?! How could that be? He's the expert and people don't follow his advice? He explained that most people would prefer to take the easy route rather than work at being healthy.

This was a huge "aha" for me that day. As it relates to being a Passionate Spiritual Disciple, the big question for every one of us is whether we are willing to put the time into spiritual, relational, and missional health in such a way that we can reproduce. And what are we reproducing? Jesus' model mirrors what we see in nature. Healthy plants reproduce more plants. Healthy animals do the same. Healthy disciples reproduce more Passionate Spiritual Disciples. A mark of a thriving community is whether Passionate Spiritual Disciples are reproducing. This takes us back to our definition in the previous section and the power and response of being passionate—only those who are passionately following Jesus desire others to follow Jesus as well.

Remember, only the Holy Spirit can bring the transformation in us that will make us more like Jesus. The Bible calls this *sanctification*, and it is entirely God's work in us (1 Thessalonians 5:23–24). With that said, we have to cooperate with God and participate in what the Spirit is doing in us to transform us to become all that God has made us to be, which always looks more like Jesus.

So what are the vital signs of being a Passionate Spiritual Disciple? Simply put, the key indicator of whether someone will become a Passionate Spiritual Disciple is accountable relationships.

Passionate Spiritual Disciples are *in relationships where they are accountable for growing in spiritual, relational, and missional health.*

> "Passionate Spiritual Disciples are in relationships where they are accountable for growing in spiritual, relational, and missional health."

We cannot become all that God has made us to be without one another. While it is the Holy Spirit's work to form us to become more like Jesus, our transformation always happens best in the context of relationships. We were made for community—to live a shared life with others.

Let's return again to our boating crisis on the water. The healthy relational environment combined with the longevity of shared values and practices together enabled moving through crisis. Not only that, though, the relationships were what caused even hardship to birth joy. Experiencing difficulties and even victories alone with no one to share those experiences is not what we were meant for as humans. For most of us, our best, most memorable, and most transformative experiences are glorious, at least in part, because of who we share them with.

I (Bryan) recall two of the most difficult experiences in our family as my dad was diagnosed with leukemia and my brother went through a painful divorce. We wouldn't want anyone to ever have to experience the pain, uncertainty, and fear of those situations. In both cases, though, it was our relationships with each other and with those who supported us in love that carried us through.

In the context of our spiritual, relational, and missional health, it is a certain kind of relationship that is key. These are *accountable relationships.*

It may be important here to name that most people do not like the language of accountability. In fact, people are so resistant to it that we considered finding another way to talk about it. In the end, though, it is not actually accountability that people don't like but instead a certain kind of accountability that feels more like judgment.

In a presentation at a Catalyst leadership conference in Lexington, Kentucky, a number of years ago, author and psychologist Henry Cloud described the difference between accountability and judgment.[19] He noted how most of us live and lead in a patternless void. Without any structure, we have no pattern, and for Cloud, the right structure to move from where we are to where we want to be comes through accountability. The key is to change people's mindset toward accountability. Many associate accountability with police work, which is judgment for nonperformance, poor performance, or failure. According to Cloud,

---

19.   Henry Cloud, "Resistance to Change" (session, Catalyst Conference, Lexington, KY, March 13, 2018).

the word *accountability*, though, literally means "to answer to a trust." Accountability is the pattern or structure that leads us to accomplish our vision or goals.

Our experience walking alongside many different people over the last couple decades has confirmed that people actually crave accountability. We all have a picture of where we want to be and see that in light of where we are now. The only way to address that gap is by putting something into action that will help us grow. Most of us, though, make very little to no progress on those kinds of goals unless someone is asking us about it.

Take, for example, a desire to get physically healthy. Countless numbers of us own exercise equipment, pay for gym memberships, and subscribe to diets that don't bring about a change in our behaviors. When things change is when we actually get a trainer, a coach, a friend, a spouse, or a colleague to hold us accountable to what we already want to do.

This is the power of accountable relationships. We will describe the environments, processes, and practices of accountable relationships in the coming chapters. For now, it is enough to name that we need relationships that hold us accountable to grow spiritually, relationally, and missionally and that enable us to become true Passionate Spiritual Disciples. Without such accountable relationships, most of us get stuck and are unable to continue to grow in such a way that we thrive and multiply.

In summary, we are using *Passionate Spiritual Disciple*, or PSD, to describe a type of follower of Jesus who can be identified by their desire to grow closer to the image of Christ by being in a community where they are guiding each other to make progress spiritually, relationally, and missionally. Before moving into practical steps for how to do this, we encourage you to reflect on where you are today on your own journey as a Passionate Spiritual Disciple.

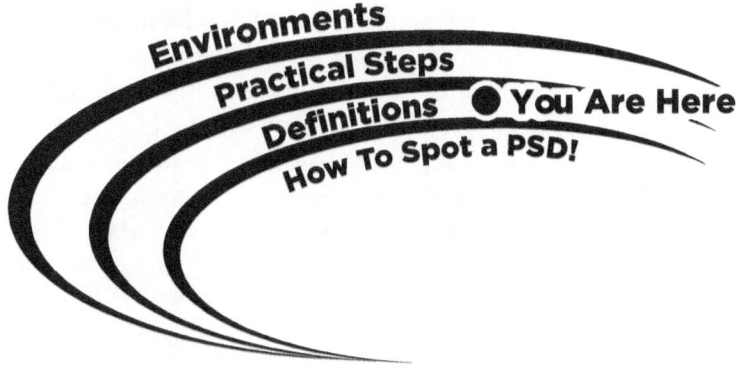

Environments
Practical Steps
Definitions ● You Are Here
How To Spot a PSD!

Questions for Personal Reflection and Group Discussion

1. After reading this chapter, write down your thoughts about your desire to be described as a PSD. If you are in a group, discuss this with one another.

2. Does anything scare you about becoming a PSD? What is creating that fear?

3. How can you create the environment every day to become more like Jesus? Take a moment now and ask the Holy Spirit to show you one way that you can abide more deeply in Christ Jesus. Start with that one thing, and keep asking and responding to that question every week. If you are in a group, talk about this together.

4. How can you create environments to express the fruit of the Spirit as a blessing for others? Take a moment now and ask the Lord to show you one relationship where you can bear the Holy Spirit's fruit. Start with that one thing, and keep asking and responding to that question every week. If you are in a group, process this together.

5. What are you most passionate about? Does living into that passion give you a sense of purpose and belonging? How might what you are most passionate about be connected to your calling? Take a moment now and ask the Holy Spirit to show you one way that you can join Jesus in mission. Start with that one thing, and keep asking and responding to that question every week. If you are in a group, encourage one another in this adventure.

Chapter 3

PRACTICAL STEPS FOR CREATING A HEALTHY ENVIRONMENT

In this chapter, we delve into the process of creating an environment where Passionate Spiritual Disciples not only exist but thrive. It all begins with a profound shift in perspective—one that challenges conventional views of a healthy church environment. Be careful not to assume that this is only for organizational leaders. This section is for everyone brave enough for the adventure.

Start by picturing yourself in a group of people where every individual can articulate their calling or deeper sense of purpose in very general terms and how the elements of their life fit within their calling. Each day, they engage in the adventure of relying on the supernatural power of the living God. They recognize their dependence on one another, they share challenges and successes, actively supporting each other's growth in the image of Christ. Conversations buzz with potential as people discuss practical next steps, viewing Scriptures not as theoretical constructs but as case studies for navigating daily interactions. This dynamic group is doing their best to be interdependent with others, thriving on the exchange of knowledge and the impact they have on the community. In a word, they are joyful.

The above word picture plants a vision of what is designed to create possibility in your mind, and what follows only makes sense if the above is part of what you believe can and will happen.

Here are four tools to couple with that vision of a life lived with deep purpose in alignment with God's heart. These tools provide a simple and repeatable process for Passionate Spiritual Disciples to thrive and multiply.

Tool 1: Initiating a Conversation through Deep Listening

Initiating a conversation is primarily an act of deep listening. You are attempting to recognize when a person you are talking with shows a desire to become healthier within your conversation. This could come in the form of a longing for something new or something more but could also come in naming a place where they feel stuck or frustrated. Persons who have been involved with training to become a disciple often use language that they picked up in the Scriptures or in their faith journey and their hunger for a growing relationship with Jesus. They want their spiritual health and life to improve, and they want to know their lives are contributing to God's mission through their calling even if this is not exactly how they talk about it. You are listening for the clues.

Deep listening is integrated with prayer. Just as Jesus did before calling his first followers (Luke 6:12–16), we encourage you to spend time in prayer for people in preparation for each conversation you will have. As you connect with people and listen to them, remember that Jesus is with you in these moments. Ask for Jesus' help in discerning the right next steps and the right words to say. Listening to the Holy Spirit during your conversations with others will often reveal deeper things that are going on under the surface.

As you practice deep listening with God and with others, pay attention to what you see and hear. Here are a few examples of how this can work.

Example 1: Person 1 is in a Bible study at church. Person 2 is listening for an opportunity to create a transformative environment.

> P1: We had the best Bible study lesson this week. I learned so much as we talked about how Stephen was selected and then bravely stood in love as he was killed in the book of Acts.
>
> P2: I love the book of Acts! What stood out most to you?
>
> P1: I just wish I was that connected to Jesus' love and filled with that much of his Spirit.
>
> P2: Me too. I have an idea I would like to talk with you about. It would be a next step for me, and I would love to hear what you think and whether you might be interested too.

P1 is a person who just articulated a desire to experience healthy growth. This doesn't mean that they will be willing to join you in creating an environment, but it does mean that they have identified a desire within themselves. P2 now has an opportunity to share a next step with P1. That next step can be as easy as meeting to talk about how to grow healthier. We are on a quest to grow spiritually, relationally, and missionally, and we want to continually invite others to join us to grow also. This type of listening and response ideally models a partnership of two friends talking that is guided by the Holy Spirit's direction. It is not about somebody trying to impress or teach but instead is about investing in the relationship in a way that could lead to mutual growth.

If P2 is doing this with Jesus and continues to pray for guidance, using the Holy Spirit's help with discernment, P2 will not be injured if P1 decides not to engage. Also, P2 will have assurance that things will turn out all right whether P1 continues to engage, because God is the one overseeing the process.

Example 2: Person 3 wants to start a new program or class at church. Person 4 is listening for an opportunity to create a transformative environment.

> P3: I am hoping that you would like to join me in a Sunday school class that I have been asked to teach. We're going to be using a curriculum that I found on the book of Mark.
>
> P4: That sounds wonderful. Have you used these materials before? How did they recruit you to teach this study?
>
> P3: I have looked over these materials, but I have not taught this class before. They thought I did well at the last class I taught and wanted to know if I would lead another one.
>
> P4: I might be interested in joining your class if you have some flexibility with the design. I am interested in studying Mark, but I feel a sense that I need to grow. I want to make sure that this is a good fit.
>
> P3: Wow, this is exciting! As you know, the Gospel of Mark is all about growing. I think you will want to be a part of this.
>
> P4: Do you think in addition to studying the materials there would be time for us to talk about our own faith journeys?
>
> P3: I suppose that would be a good fit. I just don't know if we could accomplish all that in an hour on Sunday morning. I would love to see the gospel have a direct impact on people's lives.

P3 used the phrase "love to see the gospel have a direct impact on people's lives." Using the tool of deep listening, P4 was looking for a place to start a conversation about creating the right environment for PSDs and just heard an opening.

It is true that P3 could have said that just as a common phrase and not intended to convey that they personally would like to invest in growing. They may just want to use their teaching gift. P4 knows that a Bible study alone, with no opportunity to interact around the text and apply the learning through accountability, may not lead to the kind of transformation that P3 is hoping for. P3 will need to determine if this conversation is going to lead to creating a transformative environment or not. But the opening now exists for the conversation and potential next steps together.

Example 3: Person 5 does not attend church and is not yet a follower of Jesus. Person 6 is a coworker of Person 5 and has been building a friendship. Person 6 is listening for an opportunity to create a transformative environment.

P5: I am really struggling with some things that are happening at work.

P6: I'm sorry to hear that.

P5: I get so frustrated sometimes with how we are treated, and I don't know what to do about it.

P6: I understand. I get frustrated sometimes too.

P5: You sure don't seem to show it. How do you keep from losing your cool?

P6: That has more to do with things happening in my life outside of work that help me while I'm here.

P5: Well, I'd love to hear more about that.

P6: Would you be interested in getting together for coffee before work one day?

With practice, everyday conversations can be the stepping stones toward creating a transformative environment. They can occur in a local ministry, at a family's dinner table, or in the marketplace. Many times people will not be ready to invest in joining you in creating a transforming environment, but if you have the ability to use this first tool, you will never run out of opportunities to begin conversations with people as you are guided by the Holy Spirit's promptings. It is important to note that the conversations you have with people assume relationship. How much time you have spent with someone, what things you have in common, and what shared experiences you have all define your relationship and help determine the pace and fruitfulness of your conversations.

What follows is an example scenario. Our characters are mostly fictional, but the scenario is very real. The characteristics indicate how much is known about this person and, in this case, suggest a relationship that has been in place for some time.

Our character has the following traits:

- Is married, raised a family, and is fifty years old
- Teaches first grade in a public school
- Has been on a Walk to Emmaus (spiritual retreat)
- Participates in Bible Study Fellowship
- Has been in a local church and participated in countless classes and groups
- Sings in the choir
- Has a kind-hearted caregiver personality
- Every morning reads a devotion and prays

Our hope is to see this person thrive as a PSD, and we know for that to be optimal they will need to be part of a transformative environment. As a result, following a Sunday worship service we raise a question with our friend, hoping to be helpful.

Q1: Do you have a busy week ahead?

R1: Yes, it's going to be a busy one. We have a field trip coming up on Thursday.

Q2: Hey, I am wondering something. Do you feel like your work in the classroom and God's calling on your life are a good fit?

R2: *Yes.* [There was no hesitation in the response. They didn't have to think about it, and it seemed like an easy question—not everyone is like this.]

Q3: Does anyone in your church life know that teaching children fits in your calling?

R3: *No.* [Again with no hesitation.] There are many people who know I teach at a school, but that is as far as common knowledge goes.

With the information from our very few questions, we now have enough for our conversation to fly, only constrained by time and energy. When people begin to talk about their lives the level of significance tends to jump up dramatically, and if they feel safe, they often become open to new ideas.

The reason we chose to start this conversation around their calling is that we knew that they were already involved with their local church, they were familiar with devotional practices, and they found value in serving. These are all things that are important, and if any of these things were missing from this person's life we may have used different questions.

The key here is actually noticing people and caring about their life with Jesus. It is joining Jesus in investing in our growth and health, as well as the growth and health of others.

Regardless of whether a person needs to grow spiritually, relationally, or missionally, we know that to do so in community will help them dramatically toward living as a PSD.

If you would like to practice a little, grab someone who is reading this book with you (or someone who is a good actor) and have them pretend to be one of these characters we have listed or feel free to include your own scenario. You can make up all the details you wish but should start with a shared understanding of the characteristics before the role play begins. Your job will be to ask them questions until you are able to find an opportunity to talk about a next step toward creating a transformative environment.

Tool 2: Initiating the Starting, or Reconfiguring, of a Group

Starting a group comes about once a conversation has begun. Contrary to popular belief, you don't have to have all the details figured out before you begin. Remember, this is about walking by faith as led by the Holy Spirit, and it will involve taking small steps one at a time into the unknown. John Wesley, the founder of Methodism and one of Christian history's greatest leaders when it came to starting small groups, kept a detailed journal that proves that you don't need to be brilliant to launch groups. Just like everyone else, he had to depend on God to build transformative environments. We know from his journals how many experiments and missteps he made along the way and how the adventure evolved into creating transformative environments. But not every group started, and not every person became a Passionate Spiritual Disciple.

To prepare for starting, or reconfiguring, a group, you may find it helpful to read Matthew 10 and study how Jesus formed his disciples. As you read this chapter, put yourself in the place of one of these first-century disciples. Imagine how important it was for Jesus to set the expectation for becoming one of his apprentices. Imagine how challenging it may have seemed to the people in the room with him as they were trying to work out how the future would unfold.

Initiating a group of Passionate Spiritual Disciples is a lot easier if you assume that the high cost of discipleship is worth the investment. When extending an invitation to people, the assumption is that some will say yes, some will say no, and others will want to test the waters and then decide. Remember to begin with prayer and to continue to discern how the Spirit is leading throughout the process. It is critical to remember that you are inviting people into an adventure, but not just any adventure; it's the kind where you and others will be training under the leadership of Jesus. You are just enticing a few people to go with you.

> "You are inviting people into an adventure, but not just any adventure; it's the kind where you and others will be training under the leadership of Jesus."

So if you want to start or reconfigure a group, the other skills needed are planning, initiating, and hosting. The quality of the experience is not as dependent on the place or the hospitality as you might think. We have been operating groups like this for many years and have met in dingy basements, fancy high-rises, across video technology, and just about anywhere else you can imagine. The important element is to put in place a sustainable rhythm so that you can meet frequently and with enough time to have real conversations. Our most successful experiments currently are mixing in-person and online meetings to strike a balance of convenience and closeness.

Planning

Planning for a group of PSDs to meet is similar to planning a small group or Bible study. As mentioned, the purpose and adaptive nature of following Jesus is what makes these groups so different.

Part of the planning for this process includes inviting people to join you. Having spent time in prayer, inviting your first few people requires some vulnerability and discernment, but once you have one or two people on board, they can help with the other aspects of planning.

Ideally, you will invite people with a picture of going on an adventure together in mind. You will be asking them to help you grow a transformative environment where the participants will benefit greatly. The group should consist of between three and ten people and should meet consistently for the next season. The season ideally will be at least six months, with people having the option to leave at that point if it is not a good fit.

Select a person from the conversations you have had and use the following statement or something similar:

> I really want to grow into the fullness of what God designed me to be. I know to do that I have to grow spiritually, relationally, and missionally, and I know that happens in community. Given our conversations, I would like you to consider joining me for a season to give this a try.

Once you have a person who says yes, now you have a helper who can discern with you the other aspects of getting started. Here are some things to think about as you plan together.

- Select a pool of people who may be interested in this journey.
- Identify the time and place for your meetings.
- Create the agenda.

Together, begin sorting through the conversations you have had with people. You are looking for those who had shining eyes of passion and excitement as your conversations drifted to how their day-to-day life and working with God fit together. Plan for success. Success is measured by the right people joining, which means that the wrong people either aren't invited or they end up saying no because it is not the right fit or timing. It is not always easy to hear someone say no, but remember that God is alive and well and will help with this.

Together, choose a meeting time that you believe will suit the majority, though it rarely will be perfect for everyone. Consistency is advantageous; if possible, meet weekly at the same time. There's no set duration, but typically one to two hours per week or two to three every other week will allow enough time for real conversations. Initially, you might need one or two introductory meetings or retreats that deviate from the rhythm just to help you get to know one another and get started.

Selecting a meeting location poses the next challenge. This could vary greatly and might include an online video conference element. Generally, the more hospitable the place, the better. However, the place is not the most critical part of creating a transformative environment. This also can and should change as you discover where the people of this group are most comfortable sharing and having dialogue.

Initiating

Numerous sayings emphasize this step: "A journey of a thousand miles starts with a single step," "Just do it," "Embrace the opportunity," and so on. There are so many because this step often holds us back from doing what we know we should. Getting started is the hardest part.

Several strategies are incredibly helpful here. Craft and rehearse a narrative that's clear and easy to accept. For example: "I'm excited to announce that we're ready to begin. Everyone feels it's worth trying, and we're planning to meet this Wednesday night at seven o'clock at the park. Naturally, we can adjust if needed. From our conversations, I'm excited about your participation." Essential elements include envisioning their participation as helpful, specifying a time, and acknowledging flexibility. We want people to feel they're not trapped and that adjustments are normal.

Hosting

In this context, hosting or hospitality boils down to gratitude and simply making people feel welcome and valued. If you initiate a transformative environment, you'll reap the benefits. Understanding this from the outset motivates helping people attend and engage in the group's work of becoming PSDs. If the work is accomplished, the participants' experience becomes immensely valuable.

While hosting is often associated with meals, snacks, or gifts, be cautious, because these can be helpful in some settings and distractions in others. In some settings having elaborate meals is part of honoring and blessing someone, as is the case for Alpha,[1] Emmaus,[2] or Dinner Church.[3] However, in other settings these things become a distraction to the real goal. We currently work with a team of professional ministers who have been meeting for years (two hours weekly). We have shared meals and times of play, and while these have been wonderful, there is a thirst for growing in Christ together and learning how to lead in their callings that is the most valuable. In this setting, elements such as meals have become less necessary. Once again, discernment becomes important.

The first few meetings tend to be the most uncomfortable to people, but this changes very quickly. A group of skeptical, overly busy, overcommitted people still prioritize their lives to put the most important things in place. As you lean into the leadership of Jesus, you will find the group's value becomes very high. You will also find that you can weather the storms that come when you are on an adventure with people.

We hope that you are having a thought like this: What is different about these groups? When you invite people to join you, share with them that this group's adventure is going to be not only about studying Scripture but also about developing healthy habits for growing spiritually. It will not just be about learning new things together, enhancing our lives and our relationships, but it will also be about how each of the people in the group are mentored by Jesus in their day-to-day lives and their callings.

When people get the sense that this is really about helping them take a next step in life with Jesus and not just another way to

---

1. See https://alphausa.org/.
2. See https://www.upperroom.org/walktoemmaus.
3. See https://www.dinnerchurch.com/ and https://freshexpressions.com/2021/06/07/seeds-and-fruit-a-dinner-church-story.

help a local church not die, many will be intrigued. When people have a place to explore together the whispers and nudges of the Holy Spirit, how those nudges can be applied today and tomorrow, those who long for this the most will have interest. When people shift from being observers of Christ to full participants in Christ's mission, the value of the time spent becomes enormously important.

> "When people shift from being observers of Christ to full participants in Christ's mission, the value of the time spent becomes enormously important."

Here is another way to think about why initiating the start of a group is important for you. In his book *The Wounded Healer*, Henri Nouwen helped me (Craig) see that discipleship and spiritual leadership is a shared vocation. He says that being a spiritual leader today is what it has always been in the past. It requires a community of people willing to be in prayer and under the leadership of Jesus together. A person of prayer is someone who is able to recognize the face of the Messiah in others. A person of prayer can make visible what was hidden, make touchable what was unreachable. Passionate Spiritual Disciples become effective because they can articulate God's work within themselves and with that lead others out of confusion to clarification. Because they can see God's work within themselves, their compassion guides others out from behind the forces of normal and into creative work for the new world to come.[4]

One of the most profound experiences I (Craig) have had came about in a group of roughly ten people. We were using the

---

4. Henri J. M. Nouwen, *The Wounded Healer: Ministry in Contemporary Society* (New York: Image Books, 1979), 46–48.

Loving, Learning, and Leading format that we will discuss in the next section and had invited Margaret Therkelsen to come and talk to us about prayer. Margaret had become quite well known on this topic, and she had launched an intercessory prayer group forty years earlier. I had met Margaret on several occasions and heard stories of her many accomplishments in life. To say she has had an impressive impact on the world would be an understatement.[5]

She started her time with us by saying, "This morning I went to sit with Jesus; we meet on a park bench." She smiled. She went on to say, "This very morning I was so struck by the distance between who I am and who Jesus is, that I needed to be born again." As I watched, I saw this person whom I regarded as a spiritual giant articulate the work that she and Jesus were doing in her life. Seamlessly, she shared that she had been praying for each of us by name that morning. I watched in amazement as she helped us by sharing insights that God had put on her heart. There was no question in my mind that her compassion for us and her guidance to us was genuine and unfiltered by ego or insecurities. I was watching this Passionate Spiritual Disciple of Jesus do the very thing that Nouwen had described. She was living in a community of believers who were being shaped by Jesus. She was able to talk about her own journey, and her compassion for us became the tool that allowed her to guide us.

> "The most valuable asset that a ministry can have is a PSD."

---

5. See Margaret Therkelsen, *The Prayer Experiment* (Eugene, OR: Wipf and Stock, 2007). Also see Therkelsen, *The Love Exchange: An Adventure in Prayer* (Eugene, OR: Wipf and Stock, 2003); and Therkelsen, *Realizing the Presence of the Spirit* (Eugene, OR: Wipf and Stock, 2003).

The most valuable asset that a ministry can have is a PSD. People who believe that their everyday walk about life is so important that the King of kings is willing to do life with them tend not to worry about how skilled a pastor is at delivering a sermon. They are more worried about what God is saying in that moment. They tend to be gracious, and they look for opportunities to invite others into the journey of being a PSD with them.

● ● ● ● ● ● ●

In this section we have referenced that you can start a new group or reconfigure an existing group. Much of what we have discussed to this point assumes starting a new group. It is important if you are reconfiguring a group that you do so at a pace that is appropriate and respectful toward the original configuration of the group. Important questions include the following: Will reconfiguring the group change the purpose or mission of the group? How were the participants recruited? How do they see their role in the group? These questions could help determine if it is wise to reconfigure the group. Most importantly, prayerful discernment will carry the day. Once you have determined that reconfiguring the group is a good idea, what remains is helping people live into its adjusted purpose. Just as in starting a new group, the adventure of growing spiritually, relationally, and missionally is not going to appeal to everyone in any given moment and you do not want people to feel like they have been taken hostage. It is very appropriate to move into an accountable rhythm slowly at first and then intentionally increase the level of accountability as people begin to understand and appreciate the benefits of the adventure.

If you are wondering whether there has been enough communication as you are attempting to reconfigure a group to focus more intentionally on becoming PSDs, simply ask yourself if anyone in the group will be surprised by reconfiguring. If the answer is yes, more communication is needed. If you provided enough communication and you have any kind of pushback, help people not feel trapped and free to disengage from the group.

Hopefully it is becoming clear that a group of PSDs is not designed to be merely topical or just focused on mastering spiritual disciplines, but it is a group that is designed to apprentice with Jesus together. We have been using a pattern for the last couple decades that has proven to be effective in creating these environments. This pattern coupled with the adventure of our lives has produced immeasurably more than we could ask for or imagine.

Tool 3: Initiating Sustainable Patterns ("L3"—Loving, Learning, and Leading)

There is a pattern of behaviors that we are wise to consider in nearly every endeavor. If you are going to pilot a boat, regardless of whether it's your first time, it is wise to consider if the vessel can not only go out but come back. The pattern used is designed to determine if there is any obstruction or condition that will result in the boat sinking. Experienced pilots know that this can be obvious, like something in the water or sky that is outside of your boat. It also can be subtle, like the boat has a lean to it that could suggest a repair is needed. This is true for kayaks, cruisers, and supertankers.

The same is true for piloting a group of PSDs. There are patterns that help determine if success is likely. A reminder here, though, is important. Being in a PSD group, even if you have followed a pattern of behavior that is wise, doesn't guarantee you will have the outcome that you believe would be best. There are always variables you cannot control.

Just like the pattern of checking a boat to make sure it's going to behave well on the journey, we use the pattern of L3 to make sure the group of PSDs will behave well on their journey. Loving, Learning, and Leading are the three practices of this pattern that move the team forward with a natural flow and rhythm, helping them thrive. Each of these practices is so important in the life of a disciple and a group that, when engaged intentionally and regularly, they produce growing relationships, significant understanding, and fruitful change. Without spending the necessary time with each L3 practice, a group eventually becomes unhealthy, stuck, and ineffective. When L3 becomes part of the culture, groups increasingly take hold of that for which Christ Jesus took hold of them (Philippians 3:12).

Loving, Learning, and Leading are three practices of Jesus too. As the best leader who ever lived, Jesus developed Passionate Spiritual Disciples and leaders through endless iterations of engaging L3 with his "team." In one sense these practices are Kingdom values that, when embraced, owned, and lived out regularly, allow a group or team to become an agent of change, modeling a life like Jesus. Passionate Spiritual Disciples are changed in the process of Loving, Learning, and Leading. Passionate Spiritual Disciples offer the opportunity of change while modeling and engaging others in the process of Loving, Learning, and Leading.

L3 starts when the heart of Jesus is cultivated in us within transforming relationships. You lead well when you learn well. You learn well when you love and are loved well. And you love well when your heart is well. The practices of Loving, Learning, and Leading develop healthy loving hearts that love well, learn well, and in time lead well. Each practice depends on the others. One practice naturally leads to the next. One builds on the others. Each affects the others. In time, Loving, Learning, and Leading produces the fruit of Passionate Spiritual Disciples who plant the heart of Jesus in others through the same process. There is a sweet spot in communities, and it is at the intersection of Loving, Learning, and Leading. To create this pattern of behavior requires intentionality and a few basic skills. When laying out each meeting with any group or team that we meet, we leave room for Loving, Learning, and Leading. The type of group or team we are meeting with has a big effect on how much time we give to each activity, but planning for all three of these helps us remember that all three are essential to creating an ideal environment.

Think of the following steps as a guide. Each step along the way requires you to keep in mind that it's just a guide, and it is appropriate to adjust based on your circumstances. This is like following a recipe where all the ingredients are necessary but the order and quantity can be adjusted and fine-tuned.

Loving Together

In the first few months of a new group, the emphasis is on getting to know each other. This can sound like Hospitality 101, but it is way more than that. To become vulnerable and to ask for help, most people need to have a sense that their story is understood. So it is key to not just learn the perfunctory elements such as where they work, their family dynamics, and whether they like ice cream. There has to be enough time to share stories and interact with each other. The Loving section of your time together is ideal for this, which is all about loving God and loving one another as

59

we are loved by God. People will come to expect that they will be sharing their experiences and stories, and after just a few meetings the uneasy feelings of sharing their lives should begin to lessen. Here are a few things that you can ask for during the time set aside for Loving:

- Let's watch this week for evidence that God is at work in our lives, and in our next meeting we will talk about when we have seen God. We call this a Glory Sighting! (See John 17:22.)

- Tell us about the first time you remember God having a profound effect on your life. Then tell us about the most recent time God has had a profound effect on your life.

- What is one unique thing that nobody in the room knows about you?

Be as creative and playful as you would like, but the goal is to have people tell and have their stories heard. This is just the first step in creating a normal time for Loving Together in your group. In the next section we will cover how accountability is integrated into being a group that is loving God and one another well, but in the early months a few other things are essential. The first is praying together.

Praying as a group is like anything else—it takes practice. The goal is to make time for completely turning the group's focus to God so you can hear and be led by Jesus. If this is a new concept, many resources on prayer can be used as part of the learning time in your group. In the beginning months this can be as easy as asking someone to pray after anything difficult has been shared by a person in the group, or it can start by reading a prayer together. Sharing stories can take a significant amount of time in the beginning, and prayer tends to grow and take more time as you move along.

There is one other practice that is wise to start from the beginning that often needs to be taken slowly or in small quantities at first, and that is the vision that you have been reading about in this book. It is important to state that the group has been formed in the hopes of becoming an environment for Jesus followers to thrive and multiply. In the group, we are going to be praying for each other to thrive as Passionate Spiritual Disciples. The leader can share with the group that in the months that are coming we will find ways to articulate what our next step will be to grow into the image of Christ. Not all the steps but the next step. The next step could be small or big, but each person will determine their own next step as guided by the Holy Spirit. We are not going to try to fix each other; we're going to let Jesus do that work as it is needed.

Another important activity for getting your PSD group started is the building of a covenant. This fits nicely into the Loving Together section of your time. We are using the word *covenant* to describe the shared commitment and expectations that a group of people agree are important to have. Building a covenant will help your group form and navigate the difficult waters when they occur. The process is relatively simple, but keeping covenant can be rather challenging. There is a great deal of flexibility in how you word the covenant, and it actually helps a group own and live into a covenant when they can adjust and play with the syntax together. Building this covenant together will help people know what to expect, it addresses the concern people most often have with being in a group, and it helps them believe that they will be valuable to the group. Most importantly, the time to build a covenant is before you need it. And you *will* need it.

Start simply by asking the group if they would be willing to talk about the following things and if they would be willing to enter into a covenant together.

- Are we willing to be a united group, agreeing to honest discussions in which we listen to one another, disagree agreeably, keep discussions confidential, and have each other's backs?

- Are we willing to make our meetings a priority by attending unless we are sick or out of town? If we have to miss, we will communicate our absence to the group. If we don't hear from someone, we will call and make sure they are okay.

- Are we willing to handle any potential conflicts in a biblical way? We will start conversations with questions and seek to understand one another's perspectives. The Bible (Matthew 18) serves as our guide on resolving conflicts.

Naturally, you can add other things in your covenant. Over the years we have seen some playful and challenging things added. The most playful usually had something to do with sharing chocolate or a priority of having fun, and the challenging varied greatly but one was to be in prayer for each other at the same time every day. They set the alarms on their technology to sound at a certain time of day when they could all pray for each other.

Allow your covenant to be written in pencil the first night, and agree to talk about it again in your next meeting. It is not a problem if it takes several meetings talking about the covenant before the group believes they have something to which everyone can agree. If someone is not comfortable being in a covenant with you, it is perfectly fine to let them be on their way. However, don't let the covenant drop to the minimum to which everyone will agree. It would not be unusual for someone to say they cannot come to every meeting but they will come when they can. We recommend that you explain that while that would work for them, it would be dishonoring to the others in the group to know they were not a priority enough to set a schedule. Time is required for healthy relationships and building transformative environments.

Once you all have agreed that the covenant represents your expectations for everyone, simply set a rhythm to review the covenant every few months. The covenant can be adjusted as long as the entire group participates in those adjustments.

Learning Together

Learning is another pattern to get started and an important aspect of a *thriving environment*. Get started by considering the context or situation in which the group formed. If the group all attends church together, that is part of your context. If you all love BBQ and have been meeting for a long time around a grill, that is part of your context. If you are a group of clergy and you have been meeting for a meal to enjoy friendships, that is part of your context. Regardless of how your group formed, you are simply identifying what to consider for your Learning time together. As your group develops and changes so will your need to adjust your Learning Together.

The goal here is to learn together. It is hands on, there is dialogue as you consider different perspectives, and it requires that the environment is not dominated by an expert who lacks openness to the perspectives of others. Try watching a video, reading a book, or listening to a podcast together. Then reflect and have the group point out things that are helpful. This can be a book study, a curriculum provided by the church, or a review of the last week's sermon. The emphasis is building the muscles to learn together.

Western culture is so heavily tilted toward information sharing and gathering that we often do not really gain wisdom or learn skills when we attend a class or do independent study. Creating transformative environments requires experiential learning and a group of people willing to grow in their ability to learn if they practice Learning Together. In our story about crashing the boat, you will recall that the group of people did not suffer any relational damage. They were able to work together each using their gifts and expertise. Anyone was free to contribute to solutions going forward, and they made it to their next step in their journey. They had learned together that they could navigate a crisis, and this was just one in their journey together.

Leading Together

Leading Together typically needs the least emphasis in the opening months of a group meeting. It is, however, a critical element if the group is going to be transformative. To get started it can be sufficient to reference that the group will be working together to support each other in each person's day-to-day work as you live out your calling. There can be dozens of other things that a group can do together, but helping each other grow in their calling as PSDs is the most important aspect.

Here are a few examples of how Leading Together might work in different situations or contexts.

- This group formed around their shared connection in a local church. They were able to get started well as a group and have a pattern of asking each other how it is going with their spiritual, relational, and missional health. In addition to going to church together, they each have other occupations that consume a large amount of time in their week. One works in the local government, one is raising two children, one works in the medical arena, and so on. In this particular group they each feel like their occupation, job, or career fits within the calling that God has on their lives. They are interested in Learning Together how to connect their day-to-day work with the mission of the church. The strategies vary from person to person, but the theme is consistent. They would like to be able to articulate how they are continuing to grow and risk in their contribution to the Great Commission and Commandment.

- This second group consists of clergy. Like the last group, they have navigated the startup of their transformative community, and they are interested in Leading Together. They have discovered that though their churches are very different, they have overlapping challenges and desires. Their Leading Together is focused on learning about how to navigate the current cultural phenomena and increase the health of the ministries that they lead. They are Loving, Learning, and Leading Together, which is decreasing duplication of effort, increasing the rate of experimentation, and increasing their joy as persons who guide communities in a shared mission. SLI has been witness to these types of communities and testifies to how dramatically different this is from places where leadership is defined as heroic and solo.

- A third group consists of people who love boating together (come on, Craig, talk about something besides boats). Okay, they are a group who love to travel together. (Yes, please put any theme that you desire here such as cooking, running, ice skating, hiking, whatever you can think of that ends with -ing.) Like the above, we will assume they have made it past the startup of their PSD group, and now are using their theme of traveling together. They took the time to talk about why they love to travel and came up with the following description: They love experiencing, studying, and interacting with new cultures and doing so with people they love. Because the group members are asking each other how they are doing with their spiritual, relational, and missional health, this question began to arise: "What does traveling have to do with spiritual, relational, and missional health?" Some in the group were able to connect traveling to their spiritual growth, some to their relational health, and some to their missional growth. Because they share a passion around traveling, they have wonderful conversations about different places around the world and can hold each other accountable to using their travel to further their journey of being PSDs.

In summary, the L3 pattern allows for an environment where people can grow into Passionate Spiritual Disciples and where the day to day can be a key element in their experiential journey together. What is common is the need to grow spiritually, relationally, and missionally.[6]

Tool 4: The "A" Word, Accountability— Holding Each Other Accountable in Healthy Ways

Accountability is a tricky word, and countless times over the years we have wanted to change the word because it invokes such an emotional response in many people. I have been in a group where I have said, "Our next agenda item is to talk about accountabil-

6. See Spiritual Leadership, Inc. (SLI) website for more on the L3 (Loving, Learning, Leading) model: http://spiritual-leadership.org/.

ity," and a person in the group literally burst into tears. In their past this word was used to hurt and abuse, and it triggered those emotions. We all have things that trigger emotion, both positive and negative, and over the years we have found that people have been hurt just as much by the lack of accountability as they have been from abusive accountability. So we believe it is best to start by talking about the word and how the practices and definitions we use for accountability should lead to health.

Ideally, accountability means to be responsible to someone for something specific and naming what happens if and when these responsibilities are met, or not. Hence, to be held accountable fairly requires clarity around the requirements and expectations, who is responsible, and the natural consequences of met and missed expectations. We find that one of the greatest issues people face is the lack of positive feedback, encouragement, or affirmation when they accomplish something they set out to do. It is an important part of learning, and we receive tons of negative feedback, not just from others but from ourselves. This is why positive feedback is also important.

> "How are you doing with your next step in regard to spiritual, relational, and missional health?"

There are three questions that frame the accountability needs for a PSD group. The questions all ask about a next step, or how you are doing with your next step in regard to spiritual, relational, and missional health. As people respond they are providing a set of prayer requests for the group and a set of accountabilities on which they will focus.

Here is one articulation of the three questions.

1. *Spiritual:* What actions do I intend to take to grow deeper into the likeness of Jesus Christ?

2. *Relational:* What actions do I intend to take to grow my relationships with others that mirror the example set by Christ?

3. *Missional:* What actions do I intend to take to grow in my calling, the mission or purpose that God has uniquely created for me?

If a group takes this seriously, you have a framework that will lead to true community and serious adventure together. In the next chapter you will learn more about the dynamics that occur in this environment, but for now, let's look at some of the mechanics for facilitating these questions.

For all three areas of growth there are a few standards to which the group needs to agree. Violating these will ultimately bring about unhealthy accountability at best.

- Only the Holy Spirit can bring transformation. In other words, you do not have the power to change someone else. Your job is not to fix others. Believe it or not, this is the most common standard that is broken. For example, someone might say they need to start taking care of their body. Another person will jump in with what worked for them. Chances are good that the person who is stating their next step involving care for their body already knows what they should do. Only if they ask for suggestions on diets or exercises should a person make suggestions.

- Showing respect to each other is easiest when you remember that every person is a Child of God and a Person of Worth (COGPOW).[7] If you remember that

---

7. For more on understanding and living as beloved children of God, see Wes Olds, *Confronting the Thief Within: How I Quit Earning God's Love and Embraced My Real Identity* (Plano, TX: Invite Press, 2023).

sitting in front of you is some of God's finest craftsmanship and God is in the room too, this is not one of the more difficult standards to keep. One of the ways to show respect, and this is strongly suggested, is to write down what people's prayer and accountability requests are. It is a listening posture that demonstrates that you value the person speaking, it helps you remember all of the important details for the purpose of prayer, and it provides the material for a gentle but firm approach to accountability.

- The questions are designed to help a person articulate what steps help them grow and how they are doing. When a person shifts from their own growth to someone else's they need to be gently guided back to their own growth. This is not an uncommon occurrence, especially when they have a loved one who is struggling. Many times this is as easy as praying for their loved one and then moving back to the question, How can we pray for you?

It is surprisingly difficult to guess what will be the most important theme that arises from digging into spiritual, relational, and missional health. Regardless of whether you are with a group of clergy or laity, young or old, you encounter different opinions on what the most important thing to work on is: spiritual, relational, *or* missional health. We have heard clergy, professors, and Sunday school teachers describe how their only time with God is preparing for what they are going to teach or preach, and how they feel a deep need to be growing spiritually. We have heard every kind of group talk about how they have a need to focus on the most important people in their lives, and we have heard people talk about how their job is not in sync with the calling on their life. It is important to note that often people do not need to focus on all three questions at the same time. Sometimes they have such a need around one of the three questions that all their energy must go toward that new behavior or commitment. Set the expectation early that people's focus for the questions will and should change and that each person will have different needs and capacities to take on new behaviors.

The articulated answer to the three questions provides enough structure for the group to move forward. There is no score for who has the most challenging next steps. Again, we are counting on God to do the heavy lifting, but we have to show up, and this process allows people space to talk about their life journey with others who are doing the same thing. Remarkably, there is seldom space for this in our lives, and yet within these articulated prayer and accountability requests are the seeds of abundant life and world change.

We would argue that the most overlooked aspect of accountability is when someone succeeds. If nobody notices and only things that did not succeed are mentioned, you have the recipe for lousy accountability. However, if under the umbrella of healthy accountability you regularly celebrate what has been overcome and the progress that has been made, you are providing the necessary ingredients for trust, vulnerability, and deep friendship to blossom. It also provides motivation to continue.

If you have someone in your group who cannot or will not stay within the covenant or standards, this has to be addressed. After writing for seventeen chapters, the Gospel writer Matthew noted Jesus' words about how to go about this starting in 18:15. Here is a paraphrase of Jesus' words: If someone in your group is unwilling to participate within your group's covenant, pray and ask God to join you, then talk with them privately. Often this will work to resolve the problem, and many times this will lead to transformative moments. It is really cool when the person then brings this up and talks about it with the group. However, if this doesn't work, pray and take a person or two with you to have the conversation (remember God is also with you). This still may not work, but if it does, there will be rejoicing. However, if this doesn't work, you will need to once again pray and bring this up in the group (with God). If after this last step the person remains unwilling or unable to live into the covenant, they will need to step out of the group. It will be helpful to explain why this person is being asked to withdraw and find another place that is a better fit for them. This process can be one of the most challenging and rewarding aspects of working with people.

While we are talking about this in the context of a group of Passionate Spiritual Disciples, this is an important instruction for every aspect of life. If you struggle with this, you are not alone. Henry Cloud provides helpful and solid teaching on this topic in his book *Necessary Endings*.[8] It is not a valid question to ask *if* you will need to have these types of conversations, it's a question of whether you will build the muscles to have these conversations well.

If you are unwilling to celebrate the victories and address the challenges, it is unlikely that you will have a transformative group.

> "If you are unwilling to celebrate the victories and address the challenges, it is unlikely that you will have a transformative group."

8. Henry Cloud, *Necessary Endings: The Employees, Businesses, and Relationships That All of Us Have to Give Up in Order to Move Forward* (New York: Harper Business, 2011).

We have a friend named Chris who is a PSD and leads a ministry called The Hub.[9] We will tell you a little more of his story in the next chapter. As a way to conclude this chapter, we want to share a story of one of the young men with whom Chris works who is not only a PSD but has been intentionally initiating conversations, starting groups, following a pattern, and inviting accountability. His name is Bryce.

The Hub has a group called Salt that focuses on serving college students at Thomas University and partners with the campus ministry, Goalline Ministries. They had been praying about opportunities to actively engage students in Scripture. There was already a girls' Bible study that Goalline was offering, and Salt offered to host a guys' Bible study in one of their homes if Goalline needed a place.

The Goalline leadership asked Chris if he would be willing to lead a guys' Bible study for students. They said yes, but even better than Chris leading it himself, they committed to find a student who was willing to lead.

About this time Bryce came to Thomas University to play baseball. Goalline has an Adopt a Student program, and Chris' family got paired with Bryce as their adopted student. They learned pretty early on that Bryce was a believer and asked if he'd be willing to lead a Bible study if Chris would help. Bryce said he'd never led a Bible study before, but he agreed to it anyway. No one had to talk him into it. He was very open to jumping right in.

Bryce and Chris started meeting regularly to talk through the passage of Scripture that Bryce would use for that week's Bible study. They read the passage, talked about how it applied

9. For more information on the community behind this story, see http://www.thehubthomasville.com.

to them personally, and discussed how to best engage those who would attend.

Most of those who attended the Bible study were Bryce's teammates on the baseball team. He invited them, and he interacted with them almost every day. This led to some great discussions outside of Bible study as well. Some of the students were believers. Some were not yet. Some were showing some signs of a new spiritual receptivity.

They met in the homes of some of the Salt families, and sometimes they had one or two Salt men in attendance. Dinner was provided before the Bible study. Usually, Bryce and Chris had a chance to debrief on how the last study went before they planned the next one.

Toward the end of that first year, Bryce injured his arm and was unable to play the full season of baseball. This was understandably disappointing. He had also missed out on some game time the previous year because of another injury. When they were sharing prayer requests with one another Bryce asked if Chris would pray about a decision. The next year was his senior year, and given his injuries, he was debating whether to drop baseball and just enjoy his senior year. So they prayed about it together.

One of the next times they were together, Bryce said he felt like God was leading him to return to the baseball team for his senior year—not necessarily for baseball or even for himself, but because he felt God calling him to represent Jesus among his teammates. He was feeling led to invest in them and seek to create an environment for them to grow as Passionate Spiritual Disciples.

A new semester of the Bible study had just gotten started. In preparation for that, Bryce went through a Missionary Pathway group and as part of that group identified a BLESS 5 list—five people in your life who are not yet disciples whom you give your time to praying for regularly.[10] Bryce's roommate, who had no real church exposure, was on that list.

As Bryce prayed for his roommate, his roommate began to ask questions that led to some great discussions. Over the Christmas break his roommate sought out Bryce to ask him for recommendations on where he should start reading the Bible for himself. Even before the first Bible study of this semester, his roommate gave his life to Christ, and Bryce is walking alongside him to help him grow in his new faith.

By the way, their baseball coach (who was recently baptized and gave Bryce credit for having affected his faith) posted a picture of the team huddled around some picnic tables outside their hotel one night on a recent away game with the following statement: "Walked out of the hotel gym Friday night . . . to find half of our team holding a Bible study. Not sure if I've had a prouder moment in coaching."

Friends, this is what is possible when we are intentional about starting conversations and inviting people into groups that create the environments for Passionate Spiritual Disciples to thrive and multiply.

---

10. See Dave Ferguson, *BLESS: 5 Everyday Ways to Love Your Neighbor and Change the World* (Washington, DC: Salem Books, 2021).

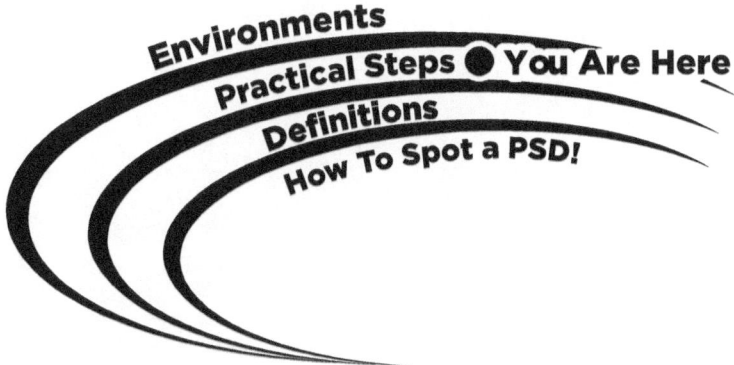

Environments
Practical Steps ● You Are Here
Definitions
How To Spot a PSD!

Questions for Personal Reflection and Group Discussion

1. After reading Matthew 10, what insights emerge for you as to how Jesus formed his first disciples? What are the implications for us today?

2. Take some time to make a list of five people whom you can begin to pray for, bless, and initiate a conversation with. How is the Spirit leading you to initiate a conversation?

3. If you are having conversations with someone interested in growing as a PSD (whether already a believer or not), is the Spirit leading you to invite them into a group? If so, how might you do that?

4. If you are in an existing group that could benefit from becoming a transforming environment for PSDs, how might you reconfigure the group? What are the implications? What discernment is the Holy Spirit bringing you and others in the group?

5. If you have a group, how could you follow the L3 (Loving, Learning, Leading) pattern?

6. How could you go about initiating accountability for spiritual, relational, and missional health?

Chapter 4

DISCIPLE-MAKING ENVIRONMENTS

After serving twenty years on staff at a church, our friend Chris began to get restless, sensing that God was about to call him to something else. This restlessness centered around a couple things. First, he felt like he was living in a Christian bubble with most of his interactions and relationships with church people (insiders), even though close to half of his local community was not active in a church. He looked at the life of Jesus and noticed that Jesus spent a lot of time with people who would have been outsiders. He wanted his life to look more like Jesus'.

Then one Sunday morning he had a wakeup call while sitting in a worship service listening to a sermon. Looking across the congregation, he began to wonder how many sermons these people had heard over the years. He assumed hundreds of thousands collectively. Then he began to make note of how many of these good folks were playing an active role in making Passionate Spiritual Disciples who make disciples. It was like a slap in the face! For Chris, something had to change.

By contrast, go with us to Philadelphia, where our friend Mike and his family have invited people over to their house to have a meal and watch a game. After the game, there is an invitation to prayer and asking if anyone knows of a need that the group could meet. Someone mentions a neighbor who is in need of a mattress. In response, someone else offers a spare mattress. Several make plans to meet later in the week to load the mattress and deliver it to the neighbor in need. Most of the people gathered have never been introduced to Jesus.[1]

Around the fire pit after the game, the few who know Jesus creatively introduce Jesus into the conversation in some way. Those who are not ready or interested are able to just keep enjoying the refreshments and interactions. Those who seem to be ready, though, are invited back on a different night that is specifically dedicated to talking about Jesus and what walking with Jesus is all about.

In that other gathering focused on Jesus, the group gets to wrestle with the Bible together and how it affects and applies to their lives. Those who are engaging most deeply are invited to make the connection between their passions and calling. Out of that, countless new faith communities led by ordinary followers of Jesus are birthed in workplaces, hair salons, breweries, tattoo parlors, dog parks, sports fields, and schools, to name a few.

Why Environments
Are So Important

What these stories illustrate is the power of creating intentional environments. As we have previously stated, only God has the power to transform the lives of people and the society and systems in which we live. Having said that, we have the great privilege and responsibility of creating the environment in which that trans-

1. See https://www.creocollective.org for more information about their movement.

formation happens. God can and does work even when environ-ments are unhealthy, but certain environments create the condi-tions where God's transformation becomes even more likely.

Like Chris' experience, most of our churches are putting way more resources into worship services and programs than they are into disciple-making, even though making disciples was Jesus' prime directive to us. And the discipleship opportunities we are most often offering are providing people more information but not necessarily resulting in any real lifestyle change and certainly not multiplication.

It is important to note here again, as we did in the first chap-ter, that we have no desire to criticize. Our deepest desire is to see the Church and individual churches and groups of Passionate Spiritual Disciples thriving, resilient, and generative.

What is important to see in Chris' story is that the environ-ments we often currently have are not primarily designed to grow and multiply Passionate Spiritual Disciples. Sermons, worship ser-vices, Bible studies, small groups, outreach events, children's and youth programs, and other church activities all have the possibility of inviting people to become and grow as Passionate Spiritual Dis-ciples. The question is, Are we intentionally focused on what Jesus intends us to be primarily focused on as we do these things?

> "The environments we create have an enormous impact on whether what we see is vital and multiplying."

In a previous book, I (Bryan) described the reason for envi-ronments in this way:

Have you ever noticed how greater focus and fruitfulness comes in certain kinds of environments? . . . A transformative environ-ment is one in which healthy relationships are formed, and in which generative possibilities are created. Within these healthy relationships, people continually grow in their character, competency, and capacity. This kind of environment fosters discernment and change that brings about fruitfulness as people are able to face complex challenges. The environment itself creates the conditions in which transformation is possible.[2]

It turns out that the environments we create have an enormous impact on whether what we see is vital and multiplying.

Characteristics of Healthy Environments

To this point in this book, we have defined and described what a Passionate Spiritual Disciple is and laid out some practical steps for how to create environments for PSDs. Let's focus now on what is really happening in the environment if you follow this process. What follows are five key characteristics of healthy environments:

- Vulnerable
- Curious
- Intentional
- Accountable
- Enjoyable

Vulnerable

One key characteristic of a healthy and thriving environment is vulnerability. When people are guarded toward one another, that environment does not lend itself to true relationship. In order for people to be authentic, to feel safe, and to develop deep trust with one another, vulnerability is required.

2. Bryan D. Sims, *Leading Together: The Holy Possibility of Harmony and Synergy in the Face of Change* (Cody, WY: 100M Publishing, 2022), 116–17.

In his popular book *The Five Dysfunctions of a Team*, Patrick Lencioni[3] reminds us that vulnerability is one of the most crucial elements to developing trust. Without trust, no family, group, or team can thrive and actually accomplish its mission or purpose. This is true whether we are talking about a sports team, a musical ensemble, a work group, a symphony orchestra, or a group intent on following Jesus' calling. Trust is critical and forms the foundation for healthy interactions, healthy conflict, high commitment, true accountability, real learning, authentic friendship, and the ability to take risks together.

If trust is this critical for relationships and vulnerability is a catalyst for trust, it becomes a key characteristic of a healthy environment. One of the phenomena of our modern world is that we spend time with many people but little time getting to know any one person. In other words, our interactions often lack the personal connection. In our work coaching teams in local churches, ministries, and other types of groups, it is always interesting and sad to us that people can know a great deal about one another but not actually know one another. Spending time with a person allows for the possibility of hearing one another's stories. When we know each other's stories, we are often more willing to hear and accept feedback. When we do not know someone's story and what makes them who they are, we seldom care to hear their feedback even if their thoughts turn out to be accurate.

Hearing and sharing stories about our lives with one another is in itself a vulnerable act. It requires us to let people in. It invites authenticity and transparency, and it is a critical ingredient to a healthy environment.

3. Patrick Lencioni, *The Five Dysfunctions of a Team* (Hoboken, NJ: Jossey-Bass, 2002)

One final element of a vulnerable environment that we will name here is courage. It takes courage to be vulnerable. It takes courage to share your own story. It takes courage to ask others to share their stories and to take next steps into becoming Passionate Spiritual Disciples.

Curious

How curious are you? When we reflect back on childhood, we both had an insatiable curiosity about everything. There is a stage in most children's lives when they ask question after question after question. This can drive a parent crazy, but it is this kind of curiosity that we need to tap back into.

In our story that began this book, we painted the picture of delightful discovery on the water with wonder-filled adventure. Curiosity always leads to discovery if we have the humility to observe, listen, learn, and experiment.

In their book *The Art of Possibility*, Rosamund and Benjamin Zander use a metaphor they refer to as "shining eyes."[4] When you look across a room, you can typically see who is curious or excited about what is happening by whether their eyes are shining. Benjamin Zander is a symphony orchestra conductor, and he is constantly watching the eyes of those in his orchestra to make sure they are shining. If they are not shining, he always reflects on his own behavior and attitude as the potential cause of their lack of passion and delight. As it relates to healthy environments, shining eyes often correlate to passion for a purpose that is shared among those in a group or team.

A curious environment is one where people embody a learning posture. As mentioned before, this learning posture requires

4. Zander and Zander, *The Art of Possibility*.

humility and the willingness to withhold judgment and delay certainty. One of the primary tools used in a curious environment is the question. How better to discover something new than by constantly asking questions?

Another key element of a curious environment is treating failure as an opportunity to grow. Many people consider themselves failures when something they do doesn't work. Rather than treating those things simply as a failed experiment, they experience shame as if somehow it reflects on who they are. For persons who have their identity secure as children of God, failure of any sort can be an opportunity to learn and to continue to grow. Taking advantage of every such opportunity helps us keep moving forward rather than getting stuck in a cycle of shame.

Finally, curious environments are like a continual experimentation laboratory. People offer grace to experiments because they do not promise immediate and certain solutions but provide the learning and discovery required to move toward an eventual solution. We find that treating life like a string of experiments helps people remain curious but also helps them tap into their creativity more deeply.

Intentional

Much of what we do could be described by the word *intuitive*. In other words, most of us simply use our intuition to get through life and through different situations. Healthy environments, though, are more intentional than intuitive.

How do we make the shift from intuitive to intentional? Take, for example, the way most leaders make decisions and do their best work. A CEO may just have a sense of what is best for her company and may even be right about that most of the time. The problem, though, is that no one else can repeat this type of success, and it is difficult to learn from doing things merely based on intuition. There is nothing generative about simply using intuition.

Intentional environments are those where clarity exists on what is true now, where we are headed, and what steps we are taking to move forward. It is purposeful rather than haphazard or merely intuitive. When we have intentional environments, we can learn more quickly and can make adjustments based on what is most important to us (our values) rather than just natural reflexes. Intentional environments are always focused on taking next steps toward desired and intended outcomes.

> "Intentional environments are those where clarity exists on what is true now, where we are headed, and what steps we are taking to move forward. It is purposeful rather than haphazard or merely intuitive."

One important element to discuss in relation to intentional environments is time. It takes time to be intentional and purposeful. It requires real relationships built on shared purpose and values. This does not happen overnight. Regular quality and quantity of time is necessary for relationships to be strong and for environments to be intentional.

Accountable

Where there is desire to grow and make progress on anything, accountability becomes critical. Healthy environments are accountable.

Take, for instance, an exercise gym where people make progress toward their health and fitness goals. While some may resist accountability and still others may avoid it, it is those who embrace it through trainers, coaches, and peers who will make the most progress.

In chapters 2 and 3, we spent a good bit of time discussing the importance of accountability. We contrasted accountability with judgment. Unfortunately, too many people associate being held accountable with being policed. The best form of accountability, though, is being held accountable to something you actually want to do but are less likely to make progress on without someone asking you about it.

In countless places around the world, environments are being created where people are growing as PSDs. In our Western contexts, we often have a limited imagination that envisions growing in faith and interaction with the Bible as something that happens in a classroom with a single expert. Contrast this with movements where people are learning about Jesus but doing so within groups focused on simple obedience and accountability to live out what they are learning in Scripture together. The format itself is so simple that ordinary people can repeat it with their own friends and family through the same kind of environment.[5]

If you are becoming true PSDs, then it is important to create an environment that prioritizes *spiritual, relational,* and *missional* accountability. As we illustrated in chapter 3 through our scenarios in tools 3 and 4, an accountable environment has a clear pattern to follow with the right questions to ask that enable people to reflect deeply, name their next step, and continue to grow.

---

5. For more on these kinds of disciple-making movements, see Roy Moran, *Spent Matches: Igniting the Signal Fire for the Spiritually Dissatisfied (Refraction)* (Nashville: Thomas Nelson, 2015). See also Damian Gerke, *In the Way: Church as We Know It Can Be a Disciples Movement (Again)* (Springfield, MO: Three Clicks Publishing, 2020). See also https://s3.amazonaws.com/thinkific/file_uploads/358440/attachments/7c7/1c5/1e5/TheMissionaryPathwayPrimer.pdf. See also https://www.experiencelifenow.com/blog/what-is-dmm.

Enjoyable

This all brings us to our favorite characteristic of a healthy environment: *joy*! This is not the word that most would use to describe the environments they find themselves in or even ones they are leading. That doesn't mean it isn't possible, though. There is joy in the adventure with Jesus.

What would make an environment enjoyable? For starters, people experience joy in an environment where they are in true relationship with others. Relationships move beyond surface-level conversations and merely getting a job done to really knowing and caring for one another. In such an environment, the possibility of true and deep friendship actually exists.

Another element that brings joy is clarity of focus. When there is a lack of clarity around purpose, values, and desired outcomes, it is difficult to experience joy because of the frustration of not knowing where you are going. Without focus, many activities feel like a waste of energy because there is no connection to a greater sense of purpose. In this case, many of the things we do turn out to be a distraction from what we most want rather than helping us move toward it. This is why clarity of focus is so important, and when it exists there is the possibility of real momentum that leads to joy together.

In connection to clarity of focus, joy comes when we see fruitfulness and progress in moving toward that clear focus. Joy also comes when we stay persistent and resilient in pursuit of that clear focus even when we face challenges or things don't go as we intend or hope.

It is important to note again here that words like *joy* and *passion* that we have used throughout this book can often confuse people. Some only equate these things with being in a good mood all the time or with circumstances that lead them to feel happy. Others only connect them with energetic, outgoing personalities. This is not what we mean by joy.

It is critical to remember again that joy is a fruit of the Holy Spirit (see Galatians 5:22–23). It is a natural consequence of being in deep relationship with Jesus no matter what our circumstances are. It does not depend on things always being good or easy. Joy comes even in the midst of sorrow and hardship when we are abiding in Jesus and in deep relationship with others who share our values. Jesus reminds us, "I have told you this so that my joy may be in you and that your joy may be complete" (John 15:11 NIV).

The Stages of Disciple-Making Environments

What environments lead to us becoming thriving, resilient, and generative? Every person is somewhere on the journey to becoming a Passionate Spiritual Disciple. Some are hostile to the idea, some are curious, some have begun, some have been at it for a while and are experiencing various depths in their journey with Jesus.

> "Every person is somewhere on the journey to becoming a Passionate Spiritual Disciple."

As we begin to wrap up these conversations about the environments for thriving and generative Jesus followers, we want to offer a picture of what different environments can look like at different stages in each person's journey with Jesus. The intent is for this to work for anyone in any setting.

For simplicity's sake, we are going to describe four different stages of the journey and the environments that are most conducive to meeting people in their current stage and inviting them toward the next. While this is not a linear process and in real life often happens more organically, there is a natural progression to the way most people continue to grow toward becoming generative Passionate Spiritual Disciples. In light of this, there are vulnerable, curious, intentional, accountable, and enjoyable environments at each of these stages.

Stage 1: Engage and Befriend

If you know someone who is not yet a follower of Jesus, what kind of environments would be conducive to starting a conversation with them that could lead to being friends?

Rather than thinking about what a church or ministry would do, which might look more like events or programs, think creatively about what the person or persons you want to engage are most interested in. Start with prayer for them and discern with the Holy Spirit a simple way to start a conversation and an environment that would make them feel comfortable. The best version of this is to meet them in a place they already frequent because it is on their turf instead of yours.

The point is not to get them to pray a prayer of faith or to present to them a polished picture of the gospel. The point is to engage with them to build friendship. The aim is to actually get to know them. You do not need to be in a hurry. Instead, you want to be present, to listen to their story, to get to know who they are, and to be yourself. It is often an opportunity to offer a window into your own story once you have listened to theirs. This is that point of vulnerability and curiosity where you are asking questions that invite them to share and you are paying attention to when the Holy Spirit prompts you to share. If the environment you create is healthy and they share who they really are, the Holy Spirit will likely give you clues as to how to creatively invite them to a next step when they are ready. Until they are ready, it is perfect to just stay at this stage with them and enjoy becoming friends.

My (Bryan's) grandad became a follower of Jesus as a young adult and spent his life building friendships with people and meeting them where they were. While he was a deeply committed Passionate Spiritual Disciple, he was also a businessman, an entrepreneur, and a layperson in his church. He once told me about a Glory Sighting (where he was seeing God's presence and God's work) when one of his longtime friends had come to know Jesus. When I probed, I found out that he had been praying for and building friendship with this man for more than seventy years before this friend finally decided to become a follower of Jesus himself.

One key question to ask is whether we trust that God really is the one bringing transformation in people. If we do believe this, we are responsible to pray and create these intentional environments, while leaving the results in God's hands. Hear this: God is already working in every situation before you show up there.

> "God is already working in every situation before you show up there."

In the creative work we mentioned in the Philly area, the Passionate Spiritual Disciples in their midst are intentional about starting conversations (tool 1 from chapter 3) with people who are not yet following Jesus. As they engage and build friendships with people, they have created a group environment to which these friends can be invited (tool 2 from chapter 3). They call this first stage group environment "Party and Serve." As they describe it, everyone wants to have fun and wants to belong somewhere. So the environment is more like a party where there are food, games, entertainment (perhaps a ball game on TV), and laughter. People simply get to know each other and enjoy being together.

What they discovered in this environment is that most everyone is willing to help out someone else. This could take the form of running a 5K for leukemia research, meeting a practical need that someone in the group has, or addressing some need in the community together.

The key in this environment is that it is the beginning step in how they build relationship with people. It is where the foundation of trust is formed. The atmosphere comes alive with possibilities as God is at work in the room.

> Take a moment to pause and pray. As you think about the people in your life who do not yet follow Jesus, what environment might be a first step for them?

Stage 2: Relate and Connect

If you have engaged and befriended someone on their own turf who has become curious about Jesus, what kinds of environments invite people into deeper relationship and connection with God and one another?

When there is readiness in someone and the Spirit has prompted you to do so, you will have the opportunity to create space for something deeper. This will likely be an organic next step from what you were already doing in the first stage. This is where friendship between people begins to intentionally invite friendship with Jesus too. This is often the stage where people begin to pursue Jesus themselves, although they may or may not have made an actual decision to be a disciple of Jesus yet. They are apprenticing with Jesus nonetheless. The aim is for this to be a shared adventure with one another and with Jesus rather than merely some religious decision point.

Unless we are missing something altogether, the point of the gospel was never merely to believe in Jesus, be forgiven, and have fire insurance when we die. The true good news is that we get to actually live in relationship with Jesus, who has made a way to God for each of us through his death and resurrection. That incomplete gospel of mere belief, forgiveness, and eternal life is what most often inoculates people to the true adventure of being with Jesus, becoming like him, and carrying on Jesus' work in the world.[6] In order for people to continue on the journey and adventure with Jesus, we cannot assume this second stage is the only necessary part. The goal is for people to become true Passionate Spiritual Disciples who thrive and multiply.

Going back to our friends in the Philly area, they simply call this second stage their "Table" environment. In their experience, it is around tables and other similar environments where people tend to open up. It is here where deeper relationships grow and people are introduced to following Jesus. It is perfectly fine for people to remain at their "Party and Serve" stage as long as they want or need to, but they are intentional in inviting them to come to a more intimate and conversational environment around the table to explore Jesus in the Bible and in the lives of those around the table.

---

6.   See John Mark Comer, *Practicing the Way: Be with Jesus. Become Like Him. Do as He Did* (Colorado Springs: WaterBrook, 2024).

This environment builds on the foundation of trust established in the first stage to invite trust with Jesus and deeper trust with one another. While this stage could certainly happen in a one-on-one relationship, we find that it is beneficial for most people for this to be more of a group environment. It is an expansion of relationships because one of the best ways for people to know what it looks like to begin to follow Jesus is by being around people who truly are following Jesus. They will see the authenticity and vulnerability of both when we follow Jesus well and when we do not. We are trying to portray not a perfect version of a follower of Jesus but instead an authentic version of real life with Jesus and with one another. This is often compelling to the ones who are newer and simply exploring.

Once again, it is only the Holy Spirit who will draw and transform people to follow Jesus, but our authentic witness can be an element in that environment that allows people to see Jesus with skin on and want more of Jesus as a result.

In this stage, we will likely get the opportunity to invite people to take a step to trust Jesus with something or even with everything. This is another thing we don't have to be in a hurry about, but we do need to be discerning, vulnerable, and intentional.

> Take a moment to pause and pray. As you think about relationships you are in, are there any that are ready to take this next step? What environment can you create to invite them into that next stage of exploration and adventure with Jesus?

Stage 3: Equip and Grow

If people you are connected and related to more deeply are now apprenticing with Jesus, what kinds of environments will most help them grow with others more into the image of Christ?

While being accountable to one another can be included in various ways in previous stages, it is here and after that these environments become most intentionally accountable. The Passionate Spiritual Disciple groups described in the previous chapter can certainly begin before this stage, but it is here that the questions related to spiritual, relational, and missional health can become a regular pattern of conversation and accountability. This can and should be invitational and joyful accountability designed to help people grow toward a constant next step in their apprenticeship with Jesus. At a practical level, this often includes practicing the means of grace (often referred to as *spiritual practices* or *spiritual disciplines*). It will naturally lead to embodying the fruit of the Spirit in relationship with others because the Holy Spirit is continuing to transform us. And it will move us with compassion more and more into joining Jesus in mission in the world.

To return to our friends in the Philly area, they refer to this as their "Very Intentional People (VIP)" environment. It is in this space where they are intentionally processing good news together, growing in faith, and encouraging people to design and create things in apprenticeship with Jesus.

Environments designed to equip others can be more formal, but they do not have to be. Most of us think of a classroom as a place where people are equipped and learn, but our best learning always happens by reflecting on how we live, speak, and act. In the case of growing and being equipped as a Passionate Spiritual Disciple, the most effective environment might best be described as a laboratory. It is a place of discovery where we learn what it means to truly follow Jesus alongside others on the same journey, but we also discover our own unique giftedness, passions, strengths, and calling.

This environment builds on the trust gained in the previous stages to develop into greater levels of vulnerability, curiosity, intentionality, and accountability. The friendships established become even more intimate such that we become more like family. We share life together with all its triumphs and heartaches. We are constantly asking questions and hungry for more of Jesus. We are never stuck, and we are never alone.

> Take a moment to pause and pray. As you reflect on your own relationships, is there an opportunity in front of you to create an environment for more intentional growth as Passionate Spiritual Disciples?

Stage 4: Become and Send

As you and others are continually growing into the image of Christ, what kinds of environments are most beneficial in calling people to become everything God has intended them to be and sending them into the world as Christ's ambassadors?

There is no greater joy than to see people fully become who God made them to be. This is part of our calling as PSDs to create environments where people are fully awakened and alive to their best lives as a PSDs in a way that consistently invites others to the same.

Our friends in the Philly area call this their "Good News Conversationalists or Designers" environment. In this space, every apprentice of Jesus is encouraged to share their own life with others, which repeats over and over again the process that we have been describing. In practical terms, this is where new PSD environments are imagined and experiments bring those imaginations into reality. As previously mentioned, this has prompted new faith communities in unexpected places.

It is important to note that in a healthy environment, being sent does not mean disconnecting from a local church or ministry. It is instead an extension of ministry that multiplies influence and impact into new contexts. In a local church, this could look like a PSD or team of PSDs launching a new ministry in the church or taking responsibility for an existing ministry in a way that makes it more intentionally focused on becoming PSDs. It could also look like launching a new ministry or mission outside the church in a neighborhood or in the marketplace. The key is that those who are sent in response to a sense of call still need the relationships that keep them healthy.

We return here to our opening story of the joy and wonder on the water. What if all of life is a playground for adventure? If the third stage is like a laboratory, stage 4 is more like a playground or adventure. It carries with it the assumption that Jesus is already in mission in the world, and he is inviting us to join him on that adventure. It is not merely about getting people to cross a line of faith but instead about calling people into the life of Jesus' Kingdom on earth as his apprentices. It is full of risk, but it is always shared risk (faith) together.

If we had trust already in the previous stages, the friendship in this stage moves even deeper to include the comradeship of those participating and partnering in a shared purpose together. Jesus is leading us, the Holy Spirit is moving, and the Father's love is carrying and compelling us toward others. We join Jesus in embodying mercy, justice, and humility with God in the world (Micah 6:8).

The environment here continues to be vulnerable, curious, intentional, and accountable, but it is here when the environment is also most enjoyable. As we are continually growing in our spiritual and relational health, it is in this environment that we are most intentional and accountable for our missional health as apprentices of Jesus. To reference John Mark Comer again, we are abiding with Jesus, becoming like Jesus, and carrying on Jesus' work in the world.[7]

> Take a moment to pause and pray. What are you most passionate about? What is God calling you to? Are there environments you can create to become more fully all that God has called you to be and invite others to that as well?

The Rest of the Story

We began this chapter with Chris' story and his experience of recognizing that despite a lot of activities in his church, there was little intentional focus and attention given to Jesus' primary directive of making disciples. In response to this, Chris and his wife, Pam, started a conversation and then an experiment with a few friends that was more about being the church than going to church. They focused a great deal of attention on what was going on in the Gospels and the book of Acts and used what they were learning as their guide.

They prayed together and asked God to reveal to them who they were being sent to by God. The Lord placed their local university on the hearts of this group of Passionate Spiritual Disciples and they began to intentionally enter the lives of students. Over time, not only have a significant number of students become Passionate Spiritual Disciples, new groups have been formed to follow God's calling into other contexts that include at-risk youth, widows and widowers, young adults reaching their peers, care-

---

7. Comer, *Practicing the Way.*

givers, and specific segments of university students including engineering majors and the baseball team. In fact, the story about the baseball player and his team we told earlier is one of the Passionate Spiritual Disciple groups that multiplied from this community.

Just as in boating, predicting and controlling the winds of change in a community is futile. As we stated earlier, mastery lies in adjusting to fit the unfolding circumstances. In Chris' context, constant changes have occurred that brought frustration as well as opportunity. As he described, the key was creating the kind of culture (environment) among their team that was clear on their shared sense of purpose and values that have led them to stay accountable to what is most important; that said, they have constantly adjusted their strategies to really impact others.

Chris describes what they are doing as one grand experiment. He questions whether, in the end, what they are doing will work. In reflection on this, though, he wonders whether that was even the right question. He names that they are definitely participating in the Kingdom of God and there are ripples of impact and disciple-making that will extend well beyond their time and place. That sounds like the right kind of fruit to us.[8]

That fruit is, in fact, only possible because of what God is doing. God deserves all the credit and the glory. God's work, though, is directly tied to the vulnerable, curious, intentional, accountable, and enjoyable environments that have been created. We invite you to create these transforming environments in your own contexts where Passionate Spiritual Disciples can thrive and multiply.

---

8. Once again, for more information on the community behind this story, see http://www.thehubthomasville.com.

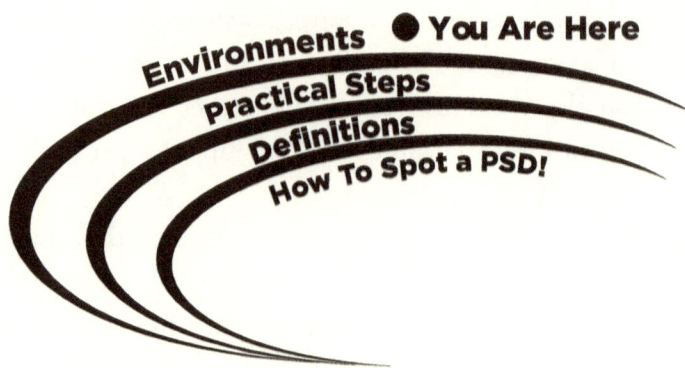

Environments • **You Are Here**
Practical Steps
Definitions
How To Spot a PSD!

Questions for Personal Reflection and Group Discussion

1. As you read the characteristics of a healthy and thriving environment, what most struck you? What "aha" did you have as you considered creating transforming environments?

2. As you think about the people in your life who are not yet following Jesus, what environment might be a first step for them?

3. As you think about relationships you are in, are there any that are ready to take the next step? What environment can you create to invite them into that next stage of exploration and adventure with Jesus?

4. As you reflect on your own relationships, is there an opportunity in front of you to create an environment for more intentional growth as Passionate Spiritual Disciples?

5. How would you define joy? What does it look like in you? What does it look and feel like in a faith community?

6. What is God calling you to? Are there environments you can create to more fully become all that God has called you to be and invite others to that as well?

CONCLUSION

What is the delightful adventure of discovery that the Lord is inviting you into next? How can you create transforming environments in which Passionate Spiritual Disciples thrive and multiply?

Our hope throughout these pages has been to paint a picture of possibility for you in your context that living in authentic relationship with Jesus and others can be a reality. While it is not an easy journey, the patterns that we follow in order to be Passionate Spiritual Disciples are actually quite simple. It is not for the faint of heart, but it is also not only for the professionals.

This joy-filled adventure is available for anyone who is experiencing the Holy Spirit's nudge and is willing to step toward Jesus with gratitude, wonder, and curiosity. It is enhanced when curious apprentices link up with each other in intentional and accountable ways. In the right environments, the life of Jesus takes root and bears fruit in these groups of Passionate Spiritual Disciples.

> "In the right environments, the life of Jesus takes root and bears fruit in these groups of Passionate Spiritual Disciples."

If you are concerned about the world's trajectory, if you long to see people joyfully embracing their potential, and if you are open to collaborating with God, now is the time to embrace living with eyes wide open. Confront fears and doubts, take one step at a time, and be transformed as you and your communities embark on the adventure that awaits.

If you have read this book and walked through the reflections on your own, we encourage you to grab a friend or a group of friends to discuss your Learning Together. How might the Holy Spirit be prompting you to grow in your apprenticeship to Jesus, and how might Jesus be inviting you to bring others along with you on this journey?

Ultimately, the fruit is God's work. The great privilege we have, though, is that God does this work in us if we are willing to take the journey with Jesus and one another. As we do so, we will find ourselves growing more and more in our spiritual, relational, and missional health. Jesus is calling. The adventure awaits.

ABOUT THE AUTHORS

About SLI

Founded in 2000, Spiritual Leadership, Inc. (SLI) is a pioneering organization committed to seeing God transform churches into thriving, healthy, and vibrant communities. At its core, SLI is dedicated to empowering congregations to make a significant impact in their communities and beyond, fostering environments where authenticity, effective leadership, and a clear sense of purpose flourish.

SLI believes that a healthy church community is a beacon of hope, especially in times of deconstruction, malaise, and uncertainty. The organization works tirelessly to equip leaders and communities to walk fully with Jesus, guided by the Spirit, through their greatest challenges toward Kingdom joy and impact to the glory of God, spreading the gospel of Jesus.

Why SLI?

At SLI, we equip individuals and teams to navigate their journey with Jesus with a clear focus and guidance through the Spirit. We help them confront anxiety and challenges with a sense of purpose and direction, aiming for Kingdom joy and a lasting impact. Our hope is to see every ministry community we work with flourish and make a profound difference in the world.

A Journey of Transformation

Since its inception, SLI has been at the forefront of creating transformative environments in churches and ministries worldwide. The journey began with ministry leaders and has since expanded to support anyone with a desire to lead, whether it be in a large congregation, a family, or a group of friends. Over the years, SLI has developed tools and practices that empower leaders to build effective teams and communities that don't rely on any single person but thrive through collective strength and unity.

The L3 Framework: Loving, Learning, and Leading

SLI's innovative L3 framework is the cornerstone of its approach. This model emphasizes that leading well starts with loving well and learning well. The heart of Jesus is cultivated in transforming relationships, leading to the development of healthy hearts that love deeply, learn eagerly, and lead effectively. Each aspect of the framework supports and builds upon the others, creating a cycle of continuous growth and improvement. Through this process, leaders are not only empowered but are also inspired to plant the heart of Jesus in others, fostering a ripple effect of positive change.

Global Impact

SLI has made a significant impact across diverse cultures and settings around the globe. Whether working with newly established ministries, growing congregations, or communities experiencing stagnation or decline, SLI provides the resources and foundation necessary for organizations to make it to their next step. The organization's approach has helped countless ministries become nimble, capable, and resilient in the face of challenges.

A Unique Perspective on Leadership

SLI views spiritual leadership not merely as a position or a set of tools but as an interconnected, purpose-driven journey in Christ. This perspective emphasizes the importance of community and collaboration, focusing on what matters most to help each community achieve its fullest potential.

Through its unwavering commitment to fostering thriving church communities, SLI continues to inspire and empower leaders to create lasting, transformative change, guided by the love and wisdom of Jesus Christ.

Bryan D. Sims

Bryan is the mobilization partner with Spiritual Leadership, Inc. (SLI) and has worked as a leadership and organizational change coach since 2001. In this position he has trained and coached leaders, teams, churches, and organizations over extended periods of time to bring spiritual awakening and missional effectiveness. He oversees coach training and serves on the SLI lead team providing strategic direction. He has coached in Anglican, Methodist, Free Methodist, Wesleyan, Baptist, Presbyterian, and nondenominational settings.

Bryan is an Anglican priest and has been a professor of leadership and lay equipping at Asbury Theological Seminary since 2011. His teaching expertise relates to team leadership, equipping, leading change, adaptive spiritual leadership, and the link between leadership and discipleship.

Bryan is a graduate of West Texas A&M University (1998) and Asbury Theological Seminary (MDiv, 2003) and has a PhD in organizational leadership from Regent University (2009). He is the author of *Leading Together: The Holy Possibility of Harmony and Synergy in the Face of Change* (100M Publishing, 2022) and authored a chapter in *Leadership the Wesleyan Way* (Emeth Press, 2016).

He and his wife, MyLinda, have been happily married since 1997 and have four children: Isaiah, Luke, Silas, and Lydia.

Craig W. Robertson

Craig is a founding partner and development director of SLI. This nonprofit organization began its ministry in June of 2000 and has walked alongside thousands of churches, their judicatories, and their leaders. SLI has discovered, developed, and deployed hundreds of specialists and coaches who are serving across the world. Craig works to develop relationships and discover new areas where SLI's ministry can come alongside leaders to help bring transformation. Craig's project focus is on large regional areas and judicatories, coach and project development, and serving on SLI's lead team providing strategic direction to the organization.

Craig's leadership experience includes founding and serving as president of Lightpath, Inc., an engineering systems integration firm. This company was purchased by one-time Fortune 500 company Ogden, Inc., an environmental engineering firm where Craig became the national technical director. He was then recruited to serve Ogeta Services, a geographic information services firm, as chairman of the board and CEO.

His passion for spiritual leadership and the pursuit of unity, alignment, and fruitfulness contributes to the worldwide effort of SLI to see spiritual leaders living their calling and working for transformation.

Craig and his wife, Jill, married in 1983 and have been blessed with two wonderful children.

SCAN HERE to learn more about Invite Press, a premier publishing imprint created to invite people to a deeper faith and living relationship with Jesus Christ.

www.ingramcontent.com/pod-product-compliance
Lightning Source LLC
Chambersburg PA
CBHW030916140626
46545CB00017B/2377